# THE EVOLUTION OF SKATING

## IT'S OUR EXPRESSION

VOLUME IV

Amirah Palmer

Published by
SK8RZ Konnect
5340 Weslayan St., Unit #273323
Sugar Land, Texas 77005
eMail: publisher@sk8rzkonnect.com
Website: www.sk8rzkonnect.com

ISBN: 979-8-9904975-3-5

Library of Congress Control Number: 2021917977

Book Cover and Interior Design:
Jessica Tilles of TWASolutions.com



All SK8RZ Konnect titles are distributed by:
Ingram Content
www.ingramcontent.com

# Dedications

After giving honor to Allah (swt) and with heartfelt love and gratitude, I dedicate this book to:

Those w e h ave t ragically l ost o ver t he p ast y ear, s ome d ue t o COVID-19, while others have passed for various reasons. My words cannot fully express the depth of my sorrow, but please know that you are always in my heart and prayers during this difficult time.

On behalf of the entire skate community, I extend our deepest condolences to the families of those who have lost loved ones. Our thoughts and prayers are with you during this challenging period. May God grant you strength and unity as you navigate through these tough times, and may the cherished memories of your loved ones bring you comfort and peace.

# Acknowledgments

*"Carve you name on hearts, not tombstones. A legacy is etched into the minds of others and the stories they share about you."*

~Shannon Alder

Roller skating transcends being merely a sport; it evolves into an art, a manifestation of personal expression on wheels. Each skater silently communicates the thoughts of their mind, the emotions of their heart, and the unique experiences they wish to share. It's not a skill learned; it's a sensation felt. While there exists a framework of style and rhythm, the individual's expression is distinctly their own.

No two skaters will provide an identical experience. Despite similar moves, the feelings inspiring those actions stem from their unique life journeys. This acknowledgment extends to a remarkable tribe of talented, skilled, educated, and dedicated individuals contributing to this project, both directly and indirectly. In the introspection of 2022, I realized that this book was my dream, and none of you initially signed up for this venture. Yet, collaboratively, we are crafting history, leaving behind a legacy to cherish, all to preserve and safeguard a beloved culture.

Special thanks to those who visually catalog our artistry: Linwood Neverson of Sk8Kingz Media, Doug Mike of Sk8 Vidzz, Terrance Glover of Triple 7 Magazine, Sk8CultureClub, Wes Jiggs, Jayson Vernon, Chad Harrell of SkateLyfe TV, Robert Dea, David Pippen of SkatePhotos.com, Roll Modul, Tyrone Dennis, Malik Thomas of Sk8

Chicago, Scotty Moson, Dr. L. David Stewart of Year60 Photography, Rogelio Valdez, Kurby Brown, Fabrice Bueno, Chuck Williams of WBSA TV, Debra Chase of Timeless Connections, KappaChris Robinson, Short Shots, Larry Black, Timeless Connections, Glennesha Johnson of DWL Studios, Scott Rinaldi of Scott Rinaldi Photography, Above Ground Photography, Sk8Luv33, Nate Wren, Queen City Skate TV, Ron Fussnecker of Midwest Skaters and the many others who have contributed and are nameless, I thank you and send a wealth of gratitude to you all. Forgive me for those not mentioned. Charge it to my mind and not my heart.

Peace and Blessings to all,

*Amirah Palmer*

# Contents

# Preface

*"Out of every adversity, comes opportunity."*

~ Benjamin Franklin

This quote resonates deeply, particularly in the context of the COVID-19 pandemic that forced a significant shift in our daily, work, and social lives. The virus's impact has been profound, rearranging life in unexpected ways. Whether through personal experiences with friends, family, or coworkers, we have all been touched by the pandemic's effects—ranging from early deaths, unemployment, to loneliness and financial instability.

The pandemic prompted a forced stillness, compelling individuals to sit, focus, and recalibrate their lives. It was a moment where the realization of not being in control became apparent. In the silence, people began to grow, reevaluate life from a different perspective, and face the choice of sinking or swimming. Financial struggles were intensified for those already on the brink, and health battles were waged with some facing lingering issues.

The same held true for me. During the pandemic, I hosted a podcast where skaters would visit my studio to share their experiences, history, and passion for roller skating. When quarantined, I had to shift and began conducting interviews via Zoom. As I adapted, a concern crept into my soul—what if this history, our history, is lost? How can I ensure our stories are preserved? Books have always stood the test of time, so I thought of writing a book, a logical choice. But where do I begin? Seeking guidance, I called Ice From Philly, seeking his advice and blessings on this journey. After thorough discussions, he saw the merit in this endeavor and agreed to assist, connecting me with individuals who could contribute to this meaningful project. To him, I am forever grateful.

I aim to take you on a journey into the heart of skate culture, unraveling the passion that fuels our love for the art and sport. This collaborative effort brings together members of the skate community, sharing their stories of introduction, acceptance, growth, and mastery in the artistry and skill of roller skating. I welcome you to immerse yourself in the passion of each contributor, gaining insight into the unique roles we all play in shaping this culture. The evolution of roller skating continues to unfold, offering a versatile experience that can be enjoyed alone or with family and friends. It stands as an inclusive activity, welcoming individuals regardless of race, religion, social, or financial status.

As you delve into each narrative, I encourage you to approach it with an open heart, engage your mind, connect with your soul, and embrace the unfolding journey—the crafty and innovative.

Peace and Blessings

*Amirah Palmer*

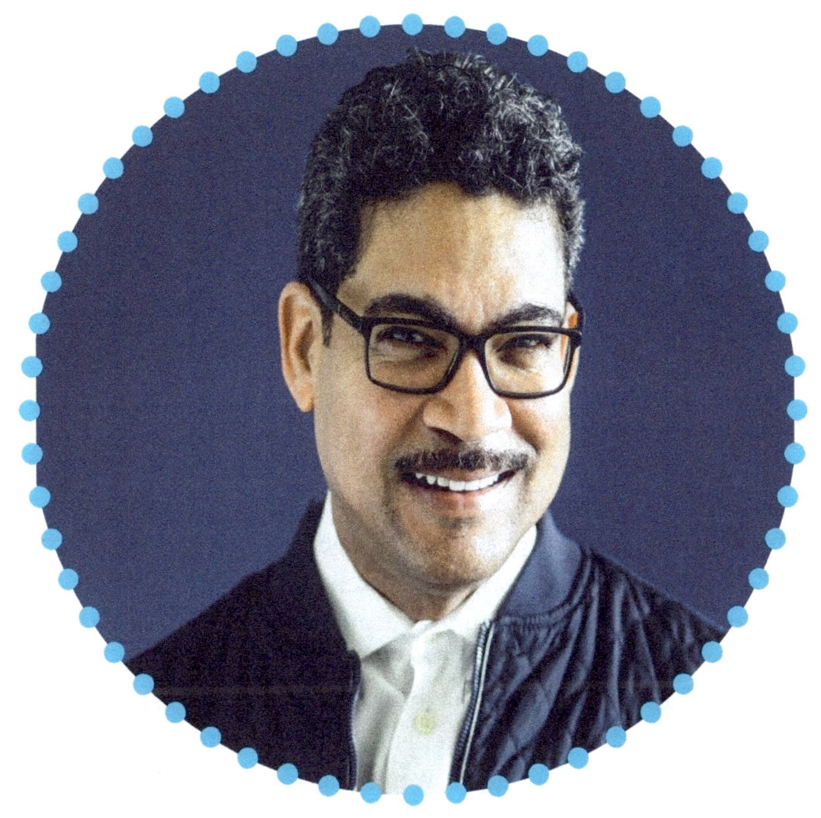

# Dr. Tyrone Dixon

Facebook: @Tyrone Dixon | Instagram: tyronedixonphd

"It is one of the first things that I truly loved in my life."

My name is Tyrone Duane Dixon. I love roller skating. It is one of the first things that I truly loved in my life. My favorite auntie Gwen was the first person to take me to a roller skating rink in Houston, Texas. It was the Gulfgate Roller Skating Rink. During that time, there were several roller skating rinks in the city: Palm Center, OST Super Skate out on the north side.

It started on Saturdays for me, skating with a lot of kids just trying to get around the floor. Then I went skating with my auntie Gwen in the evening time, Saturday night, and boy there it was, seeing those brothers and sisters get down in Texas; they skate fast, and their footwork was fast. A lot of that New York, that East Coast, that Bill Butler Jamma style, or even that Detroit style. Houston had its own style, and I fell right into it, decorating my wheels. I began decorating my skates with carpet or fur. My imagination went wild with roller skating. It allowed me to be free and connect with the music and that's what I love so much about it. Music is a big part of my world as a filmmaker, as a storyteller, and as a device to survive.

One of the best ways to appreciate music is on the wood floor because you can dance, you can move around, you can be an individual amongst many, each sharing the love.

I joined the United States Navy, and I went on to college. I lived in San Francisco. I modeled, too. Doing all those things led me to clarity with being a filmmaker and wanting to live in Los Angeles. At one point, I thought I was going to play baseball. I was on the baseball team

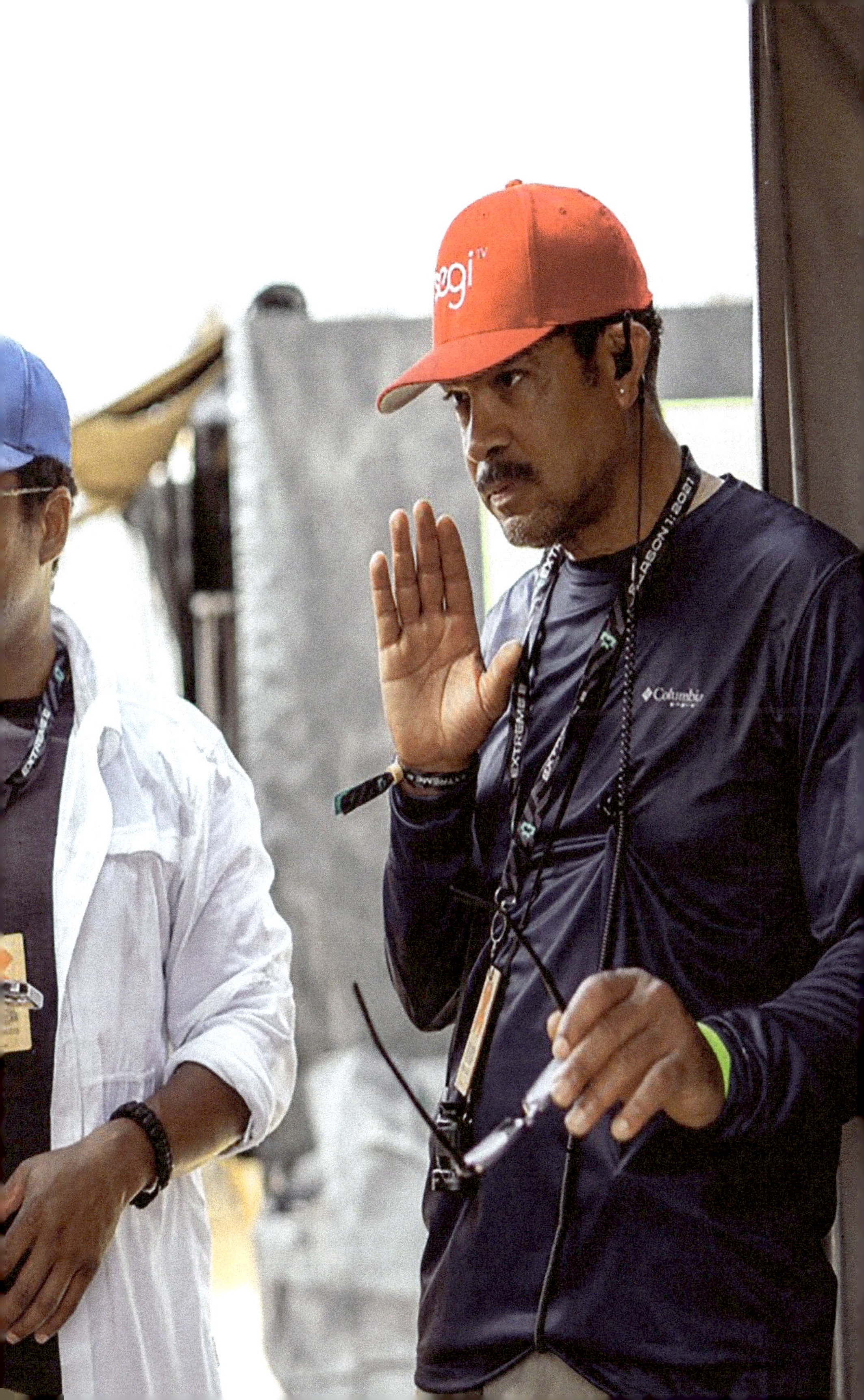
Columbia

at Texas Southern University and I thought I could pitch. I thought I might play in the minor leagues, and luck my way up to the big leagues, but filmmaking kept tugging at me and that's what I focused on.

You know life happens, and we go through a lot of different trials and tribulations. I had given up skating. I stopped something I truly loved to do, until one day, I took my daughters to a birthday party at Northridge Roller Rink in Los Angeles, and boy, the music hit me. The music was different; it wasn't what I was used to; it was a little diverse, but some of the songs just really got to me. Then seeing everybody skating, moving around that floor, feeling joy—it got me. I immediately put on some rentals and I skated and jetted around that floor like I had never left until—*pow*—I fell and busted my ass! I jumped right up, although that left hip didn't feel right for a while. I would not let my kids see me get down like that, so I commenced getting my groove back. When I got that groove back, I was skating every Tuesday and Thursday at the World on Wheels in Los Angeles. I met a lot of different people and saw many different styles. The music brought me back; it felt nostalgic.

I was producing and directing a television show with Debbie Allen called *Cool Women*. It was a show that profiled ordinary women doing extraordinary things. I became a documentarian. I was directing multiple documentaries working with Debbie, and all that entailed, and working with many of the artists I met along the way. I enjoyed that entirely. It was a happy marriage with my working on this show with Debbie Allen and finding roller skating again. Rediscovering that joy helped me through an impending divorce. My ex-wife and I are really good friends now. Our kids are now grown up—a thirty-two-year-old, married, with a two-year-old baby, and a twenty-four-year old daughter who got married on April 3, 2021 (4/3/21…cute, huh?).

Between documentary, storytelling, and roller skating came the making of 8 Wheels and Some Soul Brother Music, which is a feature documentary that I did based on the history of roller skating from a Black perspective. My goal was to share some African American culture in a way that had never been shown before. I knew in my heart that having had the experience on wheels that roller skating is unique in a way. Everyone in the world can appreciate roller skating through my lens, African Americans have put a thing on roller skating that is so unique and it all comes from music and dance.

Roller skating is a huge part of my life. So much so that doing that documentary launched my career. I was able to pitch the idea of a feature film, the concept of making a movie about roller skating, Black people, music, and the world. The production company that did it found a script called *Roll Bounce* that met my pitch. Norman Vance wrote *Roll Bounce*, and it has been around for a while. I pitched the idea based on the documentary, which was fresh. You can get a lesson from it, see the skaters, and see the audience if you appreciated 8 Wheels and Some Soul Brother Music.

I've made other films and took part in other television and film entertainment content. However, I could not have done or continue to do the things that I'm doing without the foundation of 8 Wheels and Some Soul Brother Music, without the foundation of the passion and love I have for both roller skating and storytelling.

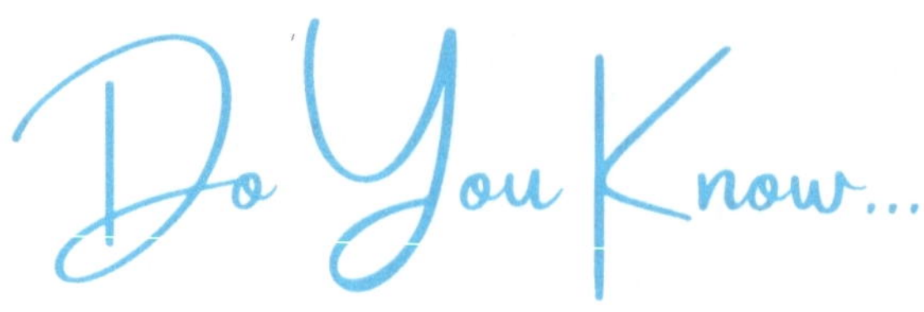


## Roller Skating Rings—the Cultural Landscape

Roller skating rinks have played a significant role in the cultural landscape, particularly in the United States, since the mid-20th century. Roller skating experienced a surge in popularity during the 1950s and 1960s, becoming iconic venues for socializing and recreation. These rinks provided a safe and controlled environment for people of all ages to enjoy roller skating, fostering a sense of community among attendees.

Many roller skating rinks featured live organ music played on a pipe organ or electronic keyboard. The lively music added to the festive atmosphere of the rink and provided a rhythmic backdrop for skaters. Vibrant neon lights, colorful decorations, and disco balls adorned roller skating rinks, creating an energetic and visually appealing environment. The décor contributed to the disco-era aesthetic and added to the excitement of the skating experience.

During the 1970s, roller skating rinks became synonymous with the disco craze. Roller discos, complete with flashing lights, mirrored balls, and pulsating disco music, became immensely popular. Skaters dressed in flashy attire and showcased their moves on the rink, embracing the disco culture of the era. Roller skating rinks also catered to families, offering sessions specifically geared towards children and parents, fostering wholesome recreation and bonding.

In the late 20th century, roller skating faced challenges due to changing leisure trends and the rise of alternative forms of entertainment. Many traditional roller skating rinks closed as interest waned. However, in recent years, there has been a resurgence of interest in roller skating, driven by nostalgia, social media, and the popularity of roller derby and artistic skating. Modern roller skating rinks have evolved to meet the needs of contemporary audiences, embracing modern amenities such as laser tag, arcade games, and themed events to attract patrons.

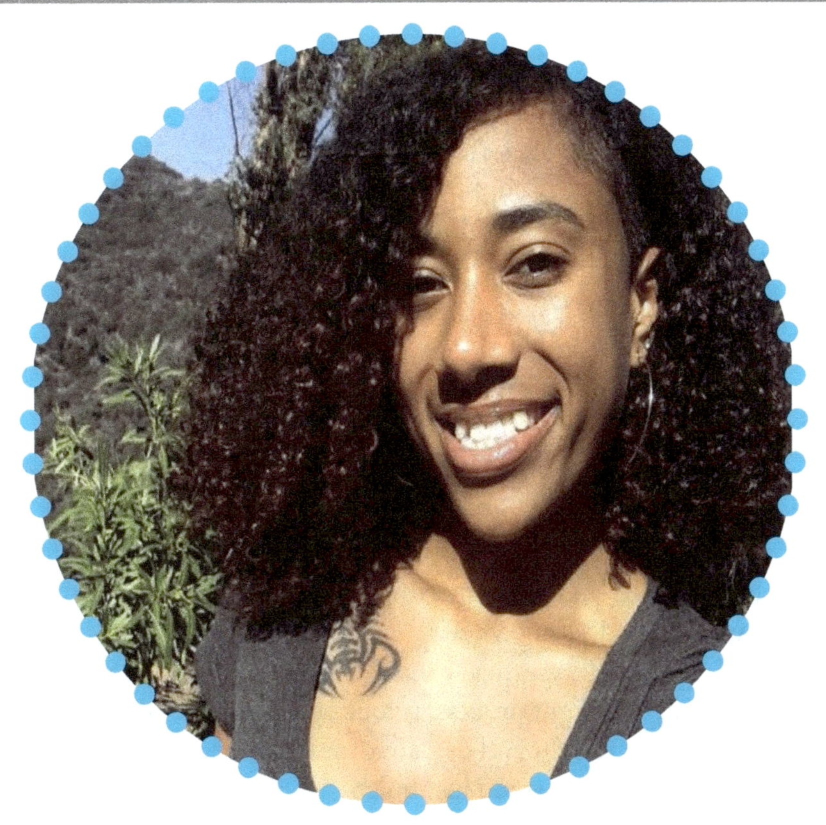

# Liliana Monique Ruiz

## aka Bily

Instagram: @bilyruiz

# "Skating is My Survival"

Skating is my survival skill. It means so much to me. I don't know how I would live without it in my life. Every day, I am grateful for the ability to skate, and even if that ability one day changes, my heart will forever be laced to my wheels.

I fell in love with skating when I was first learning how to spin. This was not an overnight process; it took so much time. A lot of blood and a grip of sweat. Night and day, anytime I could squeeze in between college and three jobs, I would just practice to music. Something about rotating longer every time made me feel more connected to myself… like I was traveling to my world, where everything was okay. I started seeing my skates as an extension of myself. That's love, right? This was more than just a friendship. #4lyfers

I get emotional thinking about how skating has impacted my life. I really can't put it entirely into words, but I will try.

I was raised by a single Mexican mom in a family of six, but now my "mom" is my dad. My dad or birth mom is openly transgender since the age of fifty. His name is Michael. I will refer to my birth mom as Dad and my biological father as that, "biological father." Growing up, I did not have my biological father around. It is funny because my biological father is a skatehead, too. He has been skating all of his life and I think he chose that over me and my siblings. It is funny how things work out the way they do. I can't even be mad. Everything happens for a reason. I am grateful for him exposing me to the skate world when I visited him one time in Phoenix at six years

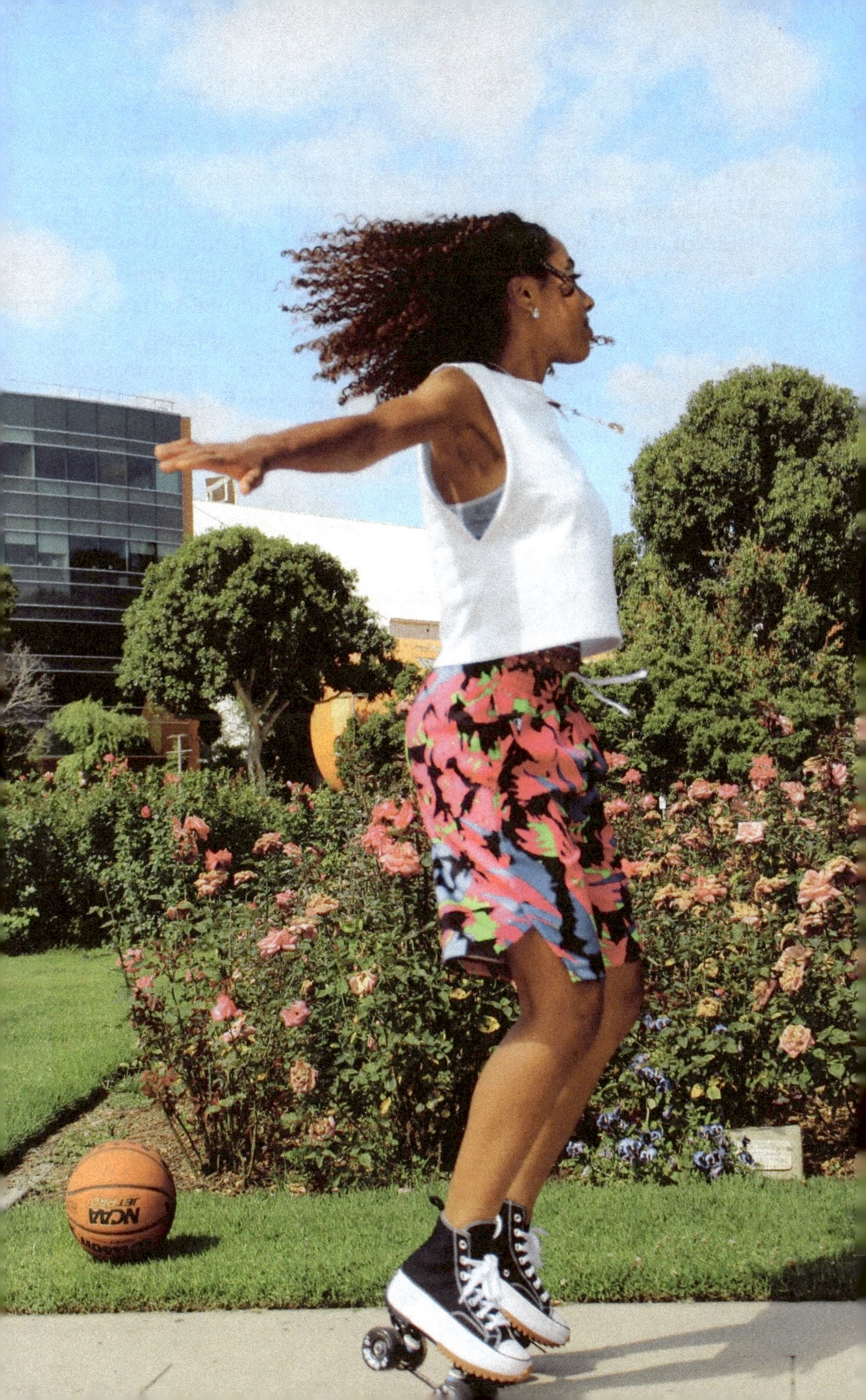
NCAA

old. Since then, I never really stopped skating unless my dad couldn't afford a new pair to fit my growing feet (I am the oldest of the younger children so no hand-me-down skates for me). My family did not have much money growing up. My dad worked endlessly to provide for us, and still sometimes light and water would cut out. In fact, for a short period, we were houseless. My dad, my siblings, and I always had a home though, each other. We made the best of circumstances for a long time. Those struggle days are some of my favorite childhood memories, for they shaped me greatly.

Skating outdoors was something regular for me as a youth because my dad could not always afford to pay for all of me and my siblings to 1) travel to the roller skating rink at night safely 2) or the entrance/skate fee.

I never saw skating outdoors as a loss, though. I was just a kid with roller skates among other kids on skates, bikes, scooters, boards—playing tag, racing, and doing kid things in the neighborhood. After moving to California at age ten, biking and roller skating became our primary transportation. Our car was taken because my dad could not keep up with the payments. That was okay. We always found a way. Skating helped a lot with transportation. I remember skating to basketball practices, grocery stores, and the library pretty much all the time, especially during the summer! In addition, when I made it to high school, I had friends who had families with cars! I remember one of my best friends, Isabella Calhoun, and I would hit up Skateworld San Diego a lot. Sometimes we would run into my biological father there. Bella and I always had fun skating. I will never forget her or our memories together skating because she was like my little sister and bestie. I love you, Bella. *09.17.99- 02.12.21 para siempre, Babycakes.*

Before skating was life, ball was life. I played point and shooting guard in high school and had been playing ball since the sixth grade. I was setting myself up to get recruited for college like my best friend, Mykal Thomas. To me, college was the way up, or at least that's what I had been taught. I was on the road to getting recruited until I injured myself in 2015 during a pre-season basketball game my senior year. Just like that ligament tore, my heart tore, too. I could not walk for months. Playing ball was painful on my knee and I just felt so depressed about it all. A huge part of my identity was changed forever, just like that. When I regained mobility, I started skating more. To my surprise, roller skating did not pressure my injured knee the same way playing basketball did. So, I became more and more dedicated to skating. I played club basketball in college for a few years, but soon skating took over my soul.

During college, I would often visit Venice Beach, where I was warmly welcomed by the skaters there at the popular Skate Dance Plaza. I loved it so much and gained a lot of confidence being with other skaters who were encouraging, kind, inspiring, and helpful. Many did not know, but college was probably the hardest time for me, mentally and spiritually. I was dealing with my sister, who was struggling with drug addiction, trauma, finances, and other family stress. Some days, I did not want to be alive. Skating really helped save my life and get me through school.

In the summer break of 2018, I worked at World on Wheels in Los Angeles. I remember feeling so out of place at first. The locals were mostly Black and had known each other for a long time at World and other rinks in LA. It was fun to work there though because I could get in free. I also enjoyed chatting with older and younger skaters along with watching them on my breaks (and shift, too, because I mean come on! Magic on wheels goes on in there every night).

At the end of that summer, a month after I stopped working at World, I attempted suicide and was hospitalized for a week. When I was released, I was soon diagnosed with bipolar disorder type 2. I experience roller coaster waves of deep depression, anxiety, and mania. Knowing my diagnosis helped in finding ways to cope. Skating is one of my major ways to cope with it all.

I see how skating has influenced my life for the better. It has connected me to so many people I love dearly, and I am forever grateful. I was humbled in 2019 when I had to have emergency removal of an ovarian cyst the size of a cantaloupe. I was unable to walk, let alone skate at all for a full month and some change. Bed rest gave me a lot of time to think and be sad, but when I regained strength in my lower body, I vowed to myself to always live life to the fullest and express myself through skating even more now. We never know when our time is up on this Earth. We never know when we may not have the physical ability anymore. That is why we should all embrace the present moment and have fun while we are here.

To this very day, you can catch me rolling in my hood here in LA. I might be carrying laundry, bags of groceries, or straight vibing down these sidewalks and streets. I am a street rhythm skater who likes to hit the rink and skatepark, too. I love the feeling roller skating gives me and I am enjoying the skate memories I am making with my close ones. Everyone's journey is different, but when we cross paths, it is for a reason. The best advice I can give to skaters is not to be afraid to fall for too long and never forget to listen to your favorite music while you skate!

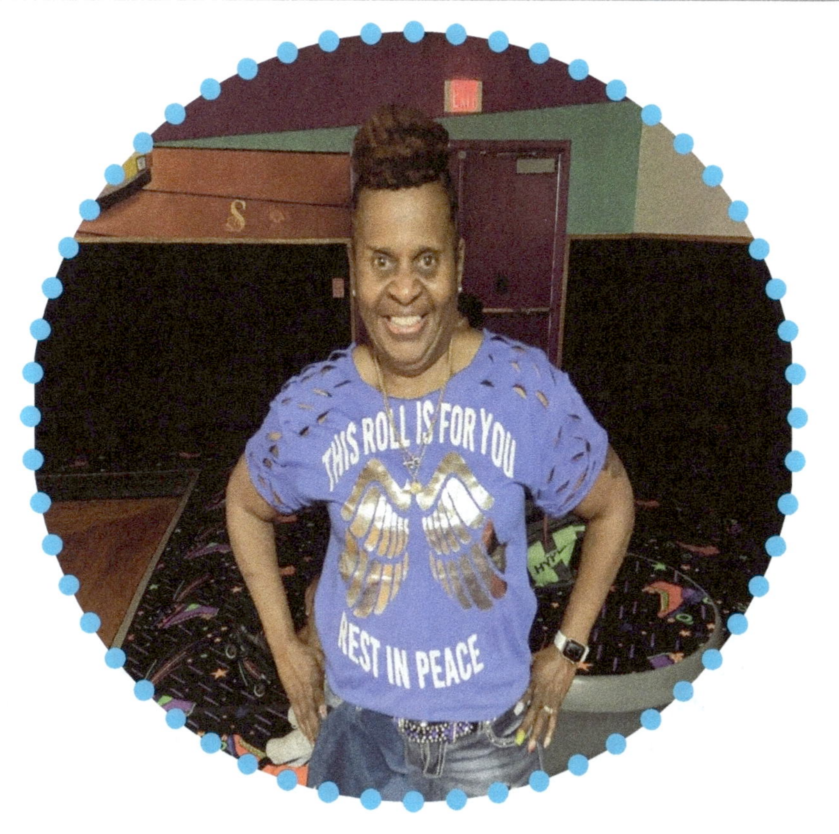


# Wanda Brown

Facebook: @Wanda Brown | Instagram: @gigi130927

# "Still Standing"

I am sixty-two years old with seven grandkids, two great-grandsons and one great-granddaughter. I love people and like to see everyone happy.

Returning to the rink after forty years and still rolling.

My name is Wanda Brown. I am the oldest of three kids on my mother's side and the youngest on my father's side. I grew up in Los Angeles, California, where I lived until October 1, 2007, when I moved to Texas. I had two daughters. My oldest daughter is Rhonda and my youngest daughter, Marcia, is deceased. Marcia passed away in 2013, which is why I returned to the skating world. I will come back to this a little later.

I have seven grandchildren and three great-grandchildren, which I am truly blessed to say. Growing up for me was not a glamorous life. It was the life of an average household with a single parent. My mother, may she rest in peace, did the best she could with three kids, and worked two jobs. I had to get up early to take my sister and brother to the babysitter's and then try to make it to school on time. I don't remember too much of a normal childhood where you get to go outside with your friends to play or ride your bike up and down the sidewalk. I had to watch my brother and sister sometimes help my mother with dinner, do my homework, do my chores, and get my clothes ready for the next day. I went outside on the weekends my mother didn't have to work. Then one day it happened. My mother met our stepfather, and he moved us all together and things slowly changed. My mother could quit one of her jobs and be at home with us more. One year, my mother

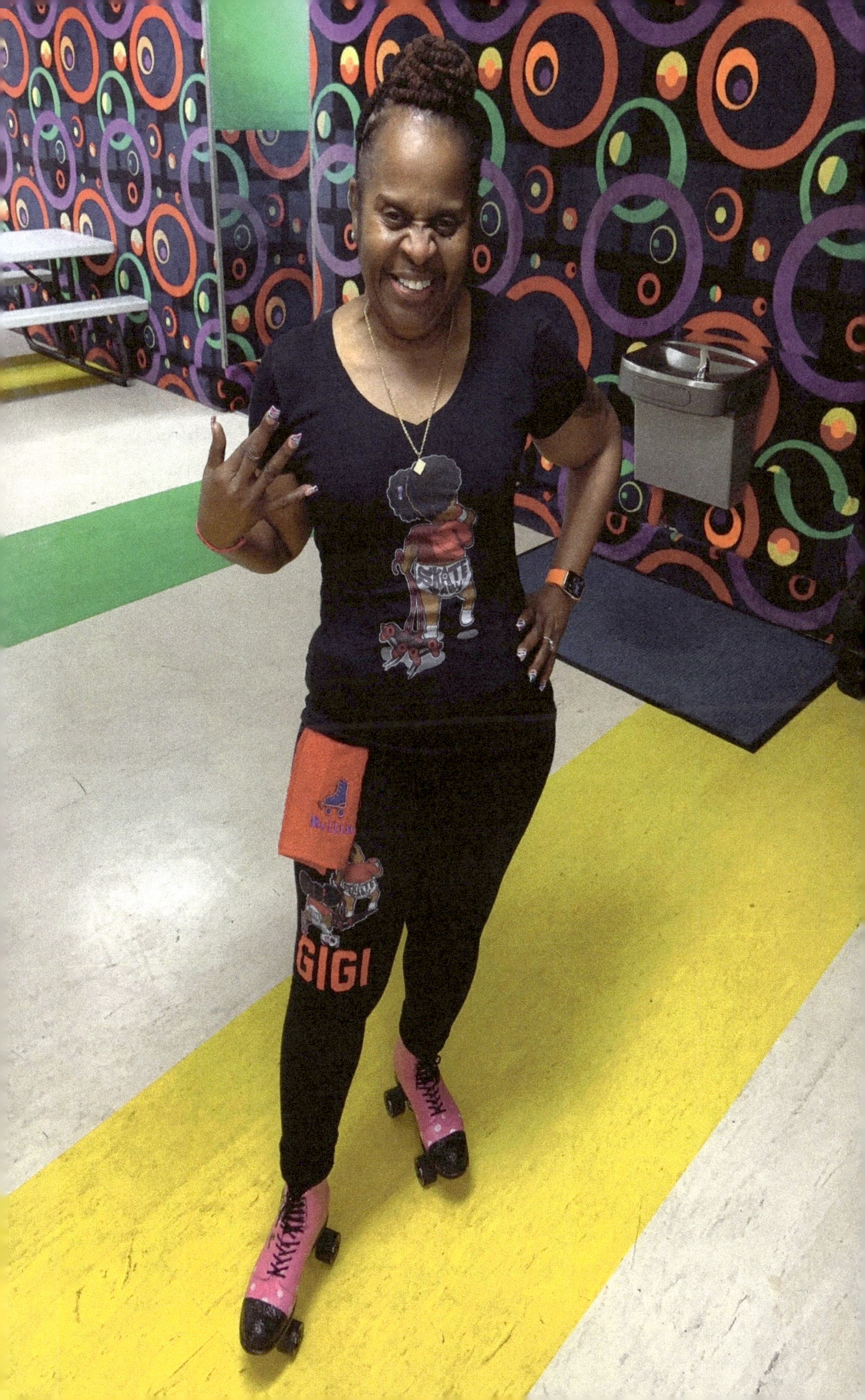
SKATE
GIGI

asked us what we want for Christmas. I told her some skates. All my friends had skates, so I wanted some, too. See, when I was growing up, our fancy skates were metal with a strap across the top part of your foot and a strap across the toes. It was one size that adjusted to most shoe sizes.

The first time I stepped inside a skating rink, my neighbor had asked me and my brother to go skating. I was thirteen years old and had never been inside a rink. It was like I had stepped into a fancy world. The strobe lights and all the people were laughing, dancing, eating and having fun. Never have I been around so many people before. Parents were there—some were watching, some were skating. It was just amazing. I'll never forget the young men doing all sorts of fancy steps, the girls with their poms, poms on their skates it was so overwhelming. By the time I put on some skates, I had about an hour before we would be leaving.

I will never forget my first experience at the Hollywood Skating Rink. From that day until I had my kids, I was at the skating rink every chance I got. Back in the day, our skating rinks were Hollywood, Arlington, and Alondra, to name a few. Thank you, Henry Johnson, for my first experience of a life of fun.

I had my first daughter at seventeen and my second daughter at twenty. The things I went through and the struggle of being a single young mother of two left me no time for fun. I moved out of my parents' home and moved in with their father. Things were good until he ended up getting lockup. Now, it was up to me to ensure my kids had all they needed. My parents were there for me and they did what they could. They wanted me back home, but after being on my own for so long, that was not what I wanted or did. I wanted to remain on my own, so I did. When I was twenty-three, I lost my mother. Though still blessed to have my father, who was always there for me, I truly felt alone. Still, there is nothing like a mother's love.

See, what I need you to know is that it wasn't because I had kids that stopped me from going to the rink. It was what I had been through, whether I put myself in that predicament or if it was life's struggles. As life would have it, forty years would pass before I would return to the skate world (my first love). I lost my youngest daughter in June 2013 and that was the day I thought I would die. The one thing I am truly blessed for is that God allowed me to be her mother and her friend for thirty-four years before He called her home. The morning I walked into her room and found her laying on the floor was the day I felt a part of me leaving and I wasn't sure if I wanted to be here. Even though I had another daughter and grandchildren, I felt my oldest didn't need me. She was married and was doing all right for her and her kids. I remember the day my oldest grandson calls me to tell me he loved me and I would be okay because he needed me. This was also the day I talked with God. I told Him if He had a plan for my life, for me to live, then I needed Him to help me. God saw fit to bring me back to the one place I would have never dreamed of coming back to—my first true love of skating.

Maybe somebody or someone you know is struggling with a loss and feels the way I did. I pray this small piece of my testimony will give you hope. Not only did God bring me back to the one place I fell in love with, but He also placed two angels in my path to keep me here: Freda and Karen. I was ready to give up after about a month or two. I was tired of falling every Sunday. I felt like I was too old and couldn't do this. However, Karen and Freda grabbed me by the hand and supported me until I could hold myself up. They are my angels. If God had not had a plan for my life, I probably wouldn't be here today. God gave me the tools to deal with my daughter's death, and it was up to me to use them. I can't thank God enough for not giving up on me or allowing me to give up on myself. I also thank Him for placing these angels in my life who didn't give up on me, either.

I have been back skating for almost eight years. Skating helped me to deal with my tragedy and now it is a way of life for me. I truly enjoy skating and now my grandkids and great-grandson do also. My daughter will soon join us and it will be a family affair. Therefore, skating will remain a part of my life until God calls me home. Skating not only helped to save my life, it gave me hope, courage, and strength to carry on when I thought I was out of hope. Trust in God, for He can do all things but fail you. God not only saved me, but He also blessed me with angels, gave me a beautiful SK8 family, and one of the greatest skate clubs you can imagine—Texas Wood Rydrz, my family for life.

I want to elaborate a bit on my Wood Rydrz family. Let me first thank my son (Tiger) for suggesting to Sweet P (Patricia) that she call me. When I asked to start up a chapter in Texas, my only request was to do it my way. The CEO, Sweet P, gave me the green light, and I handpicked each member in the Texas Wood Rydrz Skate Club and we have become a family since 2019. We are nowhere near a perfect skate club family, but we come together as one when needed. We are not like your usual skate crew. We are probably the first mature (as in age) skate club. To be part of Texas Wood Rydrz, you must be fifty or older. The second qualification is there is a waiting period; if you truly want to be a part of our club, time will tell. These are the main two qualifications to become a Texas Wood Rydrz. What I love about my crew is that we may not agree on everything, but when it comes down to it, we will talk about it and move on. We are just like politicians, too. We vote on everything. There are no big I's or little t's. When it's time to show up, my crew is there and they show out. Meaning we try to get the crowd involved in everything we are doing.

Texas Wood Rydrz isn't alone. There are California, Northern California, Denver, Atlanta, Chicago, London and please let me not forget to mention our newest skate club family, Arizona. When we all get together, we have such a good time. Whether we're doing an event or just socializing, we do it big. It feels so good to be a part of something where you can be yourself, express yourself, and have fun all at the same time. Well, that's what we do as a family here in the Wood Rydrz Skate Club. The Wood Rydrz is a skate club that believes in giving back and helping others, which is what attracted me to them after talking to Sweet P. I am grateful to be a part of such a beautiful family. I truly thank her for this opportunity.

Before I end, let me say this. Yes, there are things in my past I am not proud of, but it is not for this anthology. I am not ashamed of where I have been or of my past. If it had not been for my past, I would not have had anything to look forward to in my future. I was allowed to live through my good, my bad, and my ugly and now I can love myself and live out my best life.

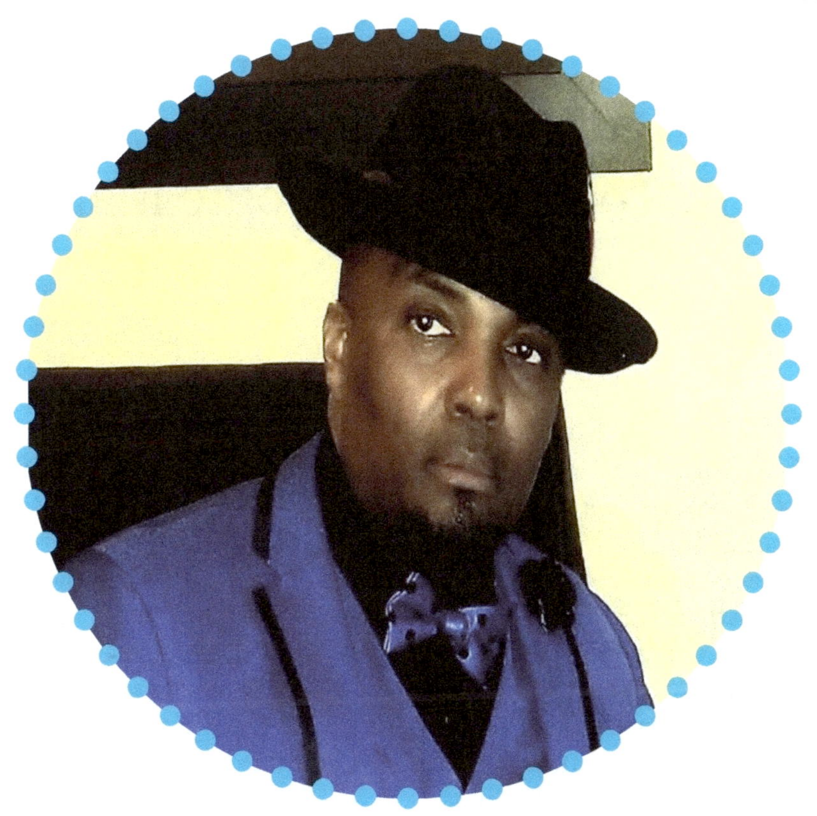

Rickey Davis

aka Tip Toe

Facebook: @Rickey Davis | Instagram: @rickeydavisclassicman

# "Tip Toe and the Boogie Man"

"Well, I got a brand new pair of roller skates and they have metal wheels. Yes, Granddaddy, they clamp to my shoes and they have a key."

That was my reply when my grandfather asked, "What did you get for Christmas, Tickey?"

The year was 1971 and a boy's life was in full effect at eight years old. I was born and raised in the small cotton and peanut town of Edison, Georgia, but new adventures were on the horizon because my mother moved the family to Jacksonville, Florida, a city with paved streets and more than one school.

My Grandfather, Willie D. Davis, got me my very first set of wheels, following the murder of my father in 1969. Yep, it was a Big Wheel. He also bought me a 1969 model Corvette, and it had some pretty cool rally sport wheels. The Big Wheel had one ginormous wheel, but my Corvette had four wheels. You see, life for a young boy back then was about hot wheels. Wheels attracted girls and wheels attract girls still today. I guess some things will never change. My main wheel was a bicycle, and it was cool because it had two wheels. Life was good because my new skates took me places I could now join up with my friends in my neighborhood. Kids were everywhere, including the streets, rolling on eight wheels made of metal. To make sure my skates were tight enough on my feet, I would tighten them using a skate key. This key was kept around my neck, attached by a shoestring. Surely, we all looked like Frankenstein's monster, trying to stand upright for our first time skating. I wasn't alone in the game of "fall and get back up." I kept asking, "Why is the ground jumping up and hitting me on my

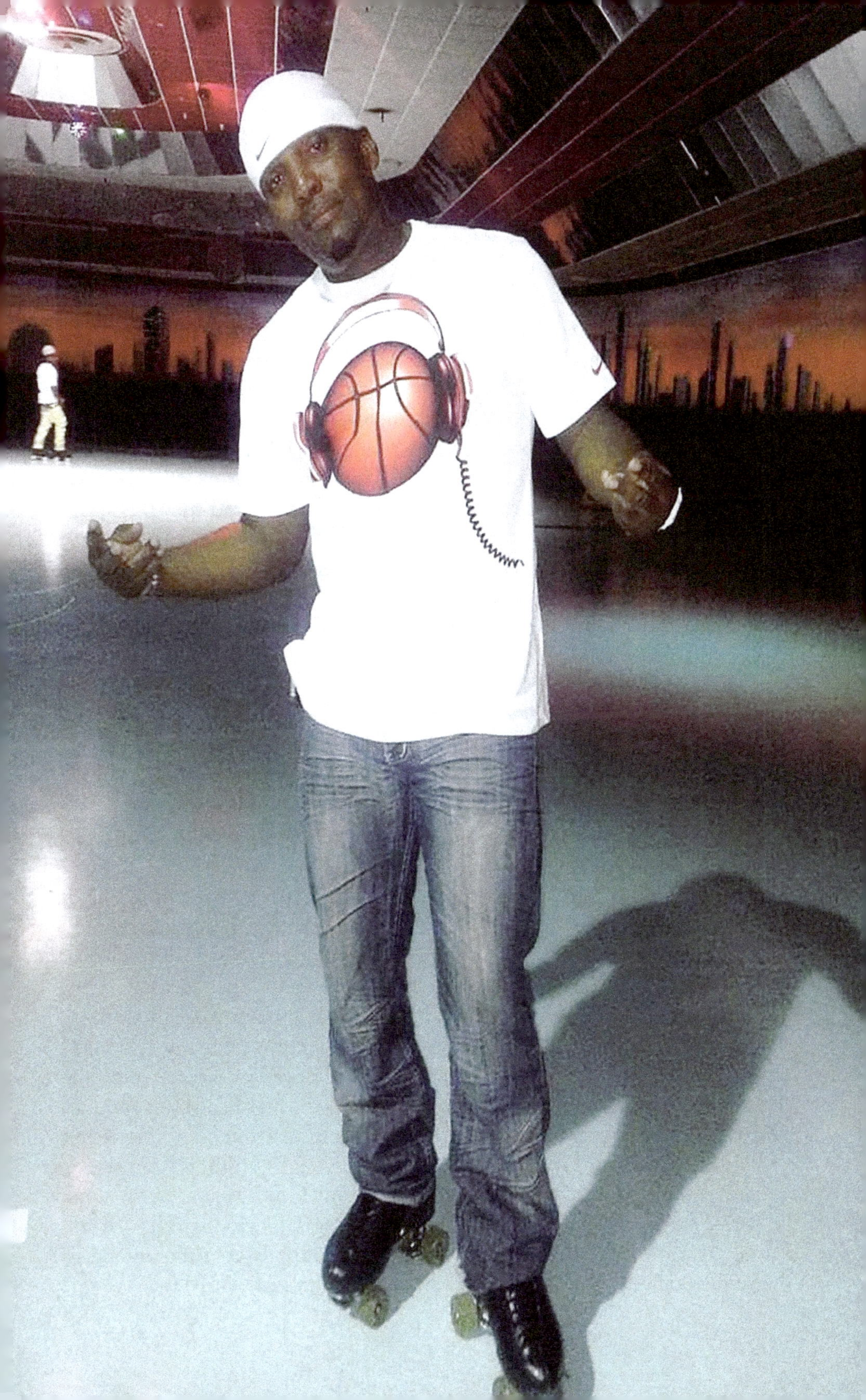

elbows and knees?" Concrete is a hard surface, but concrete heated by the sunlight in Florida will train you quickly to remain upright. Within a month, my skate life was put on hold because I lost that metal key from around my neck. Oh well, that's life. I would quietly Tip Toe back to my Big Wheel.

Disco was all the rage in 1976, and it had a major superstar. KC and The Sunshine Band and his music were the new feel-good to my thirteen-year-old ears. The disco sound didn't go unnoticed by my older neighbor across the street, either. One evening, she blasted her record player featuring KC'S hit song, "I'm Your Boogie Man" and it was heard all the way to the state of Georgia. Of course, I went over to have her turn it down, but I got turned up instead. She invited me to go with her and her two brothers to a skating rink. Into the station wagon we gathered, and KC was on the radio dial. I was truly living the life. When we got inside the rink, music greeted us and it had a familiar tone to it. Yep, it was "I'm Your Boogie Man" and it was bellowing throughout the rink everywhere. Yes, sir, I became a Boogie Man on eight wheels that night. Needless to tell you, there was dust from the wood floor spurning about and turning everyone's Afro ash white. It was amazing and so it was on this night the start of my roller-skating evolution. I noticed something different about the skates that night. They were now made of leather and the wheels were some kind of hard plastic. Wait, it got better. *You mean my mom doesn't have to buy me these skates and I don't need a metal key to carry around my neck?*

Disco remained in full effect, but I wouldn't set foot in a pair of roller skates again until 1977. Word came that a new skating rink was going to be built in my neighborhood of Sherwood Forest. Jacksonville's Black businessman, Harold Gibson, opened Skate City, and it became a holy shrine for all of north Jacksonville. Skate City was also a Saturday afternoon drop-off and getaway for my mom and many others. She could drop off all four of her kids, then run and take care of errands. Every Saturday morning, my mother heard this familiar cry. "Momma, can we please go to the skating rink?" Roller skating became the Saturday activity each week throughout junior and senior high school. I would venture to Skate City my senior year at night alone with my three buddies: Tyrone Williams (Yogi), David Griffith (Griff), me (Nature Boy), and Fred Horace. Fred didn't have a nickname, so we just called him Fred. Together we were "the Hawk Men." We got this name because we were always hawking. Definition of hawking: "to frequent a place way too often." The four of us would mow grass throughout Sherwood for $5.00. We would also search in ditches to find Coke bottles to sell for a dime apiece. We needed to make enough to get inside the skating rink at $5 and nothing was going to stop us. We had a goal to earn at least $10.00 apiece so that we would have enough money to buy a barbecue sandwich from Mr. K'S Bar-B-Q for the long walk home.

This routine became my life story every Saturday and until I graduated high school in 1981. The day after graduating high school, I left Jacksonville, Florida, and moved to Houston for college. I never saw or heard about a skating rink again for twenty-five years. I honestly never thought about skating again because my focus was on school and my new adult life. Adult life brought me to age forty-two in 2006 and along with fatherhood, skating was a distant memory. My six-year-old son attended a birthday party in 2006 and came home and told me about it.

"What did you say, son? Skating rink, but where?"

I told my son that he had to be mistaken because I had lived in Houston for twenty-five years and I have never seen a skating rink ever. Well, I went in search of this rink and found Skate Central in Stafford, Texas. I literally cried at the site of the building, as I reflected on the days of good times and my childhood friends. I soon met members of The Space City Rollers and they told me all about this underground culture, which I knew nothing about at the time. They were style skaters who performed some of the most incredible dance routines on skates. I was invited to come out to Sunday adult night skating at Almeda Skating Rink. There I saw, in this other world, but right here on Earth. The rink was packed and everyone was dancing, but on skates. This was too much to believe. "What in the heck is an adult night?" I asked. "What in the heck is the Crazy Legs?"

I witnessed something very special that night in 2006, and I was hooked. They invited me to travel with them to Atlanta, Georgia, to the Skate-A-Thon in 2006. It was the most heartwarming gathering I had ever experienced. I saw pure love for roller skating. I witnessed human camaraderie like I'd never witnessed before. It was on full display and by people who mostly look like me. I made a commitment that weekend to keep this treasured art form alive. I've had a wonderful opportunity to visit several cities and skate in many rinks over the years. Now my attention is to make sure the world knows about this incredible art and the people who have kept their childhood fulfillment alive. I will not stop skating until the day I'm called to trade in my eight wheels for two wings. Eight is enough and SK8-ing gives me such great feelings when I'm rolling through life and serving my purpose.

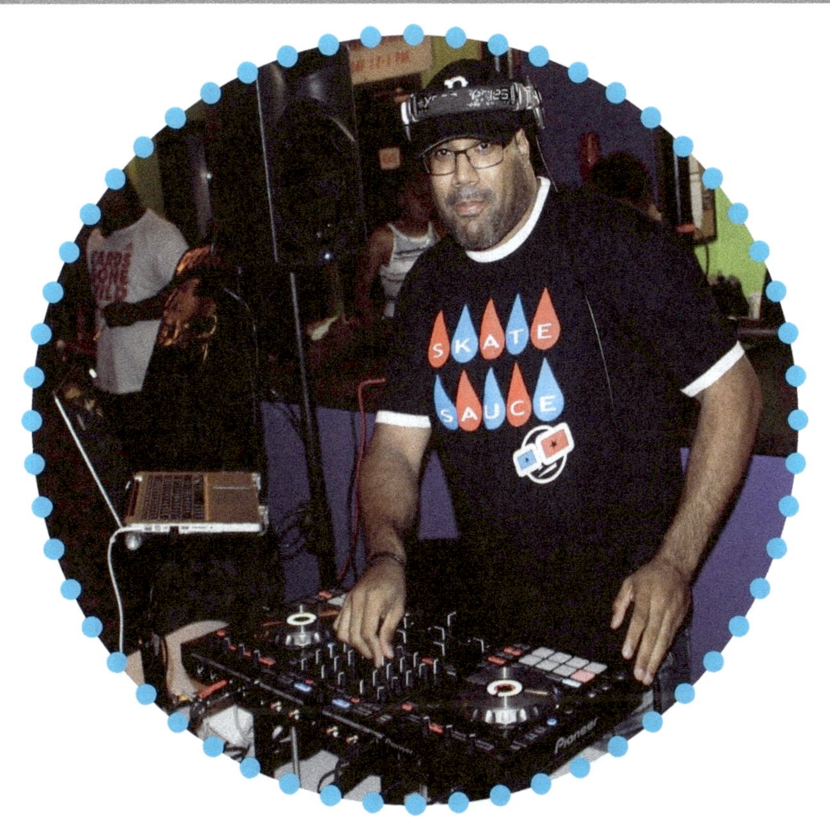


# Joe Bowen

## aka DJ Joe Bowen

Facebook: @DJ Joe Bowen | Instagram: @djjoebowen

# "Skating Has Brought Together Three Things I love."

I remember going to the roller rink as a kid and skating or "staying up" without falling. The more I went, the more confident I became. I wouldn't say that I went skating every week but at least once or twice a month with my school or youth group from church. So saying I fell in love with skating at the time wasn't the case. I loved skating when I went to the rink. It was also fun hanging out with friends, and who could ever forget the famous hot dog, chip, and pop combo? What about the rink nachos? I remember the rink playing all the music that was popular on the radio and later when music television channels and videos were the thing. Waiting on my favorite song so I would really skate fast and sing along. Wow, great memories! If you would've told me back then as a kid that I would travel all over the United States and beyond to skate, I would have told you probably not. So I had a real passion for music from a young age. My parents always had music playing in the house. On holidays, everybody was at the house and a longtime family friend who was also a DJ would always set up and play music for hours. So I would always sit right there and watch. So I wanted to DJ, and I started at thirteen years old, learning how to be a DJ. So now when I went skating, I paid more attention to the music. If you would've told me then as a kid that one day I would travel all over the United States and beyond playing music for people to skate to, I would've told you, "I doubt it."

So the two things that I enjoyed and loved to do finally came together. How, you ask? I worked at a roller rink as a DJ and started on the gospel and family sessions. So now I skated three to four times

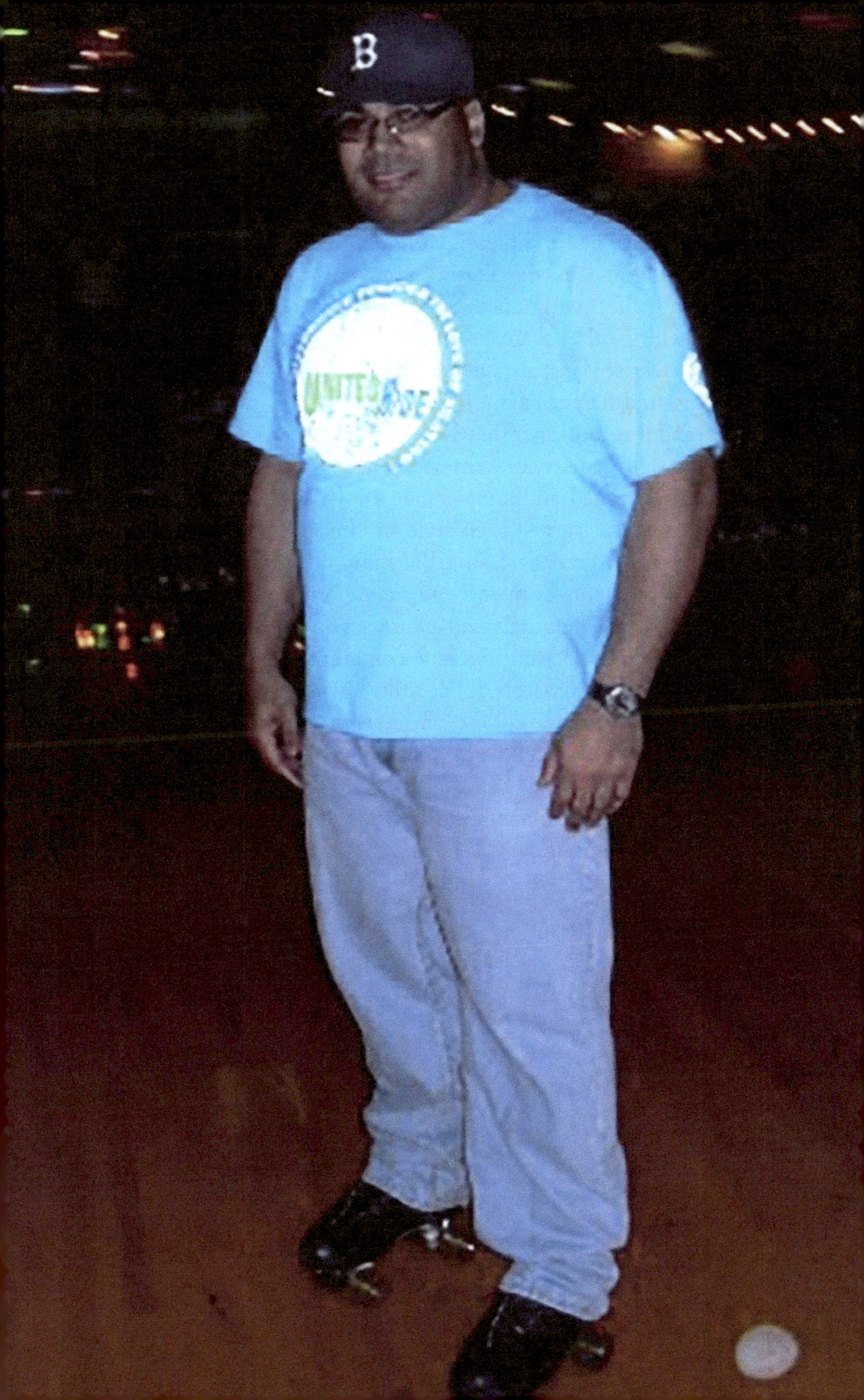

a week. It was at that point that I really fell in love with skating. I had the best of both worlds every week. So from that point on to the present, I have had the pleasure of doing both of the things I love to do—skating and music. Skating for me is an outlet for whatever is going on in life, good or bad. Skating is also great exercise. Being a DJ and watching other skaters on the floor getting it in and having their outlet or release is just as much rewarding. As a skater, it was fascinating traveling to different parts of the United States, watching other skate styles, and learning what they were. As a DJ, it was fascinating and fun, learning what skate styles went with what type of music. So, being from Chicago, I learned and knew about the JB skating style. One of the first cities that I learned their style and music and they took me in as one of their own was St. Louis. Big shout out to St. Louis. That's why I refer to St. Louis as my second skate home. Skating and the skate community have definitely had an impact on my life and I believe that I have had an impact on the skate community as well. I thank all the skaters, skate coordinators, roller rinks (owners and managers) for the support over the years and the continued support. The greatest impact that skating has had on my life was meeting my wife, Angela, in Dallas, Texas, at the Skate Fair Classic. It was totally unexpected. We struck up a conversation at breakfast following the main event session which I had deejayed and the rest is history. So skating has brought together three things that I love.

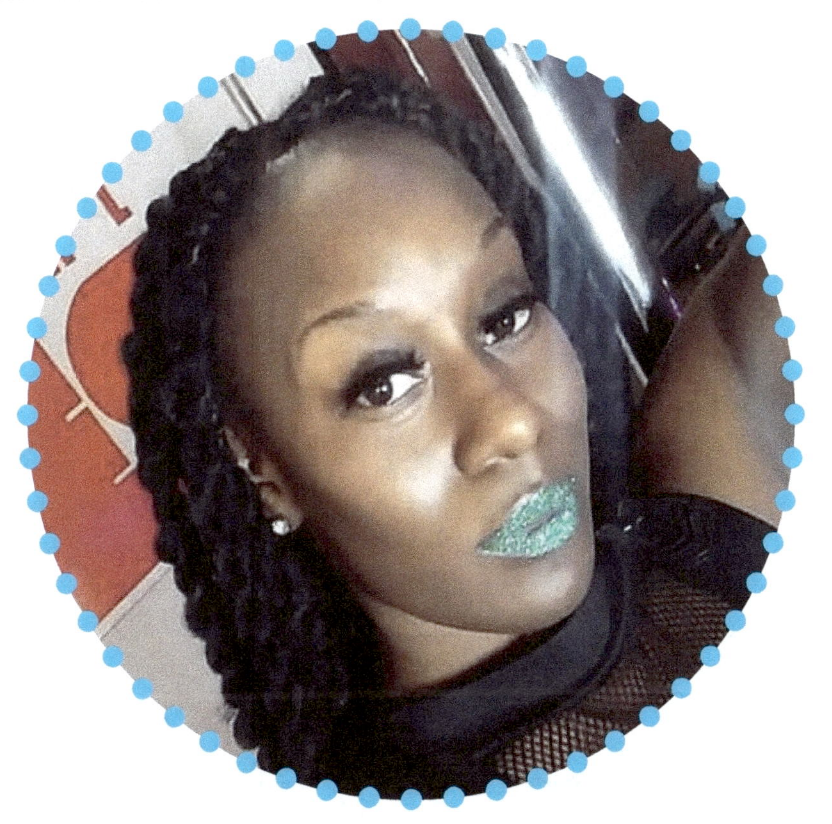

## Denise Wesley

### aka DanceLegz

Facebook: @Denise Wesley | Instagram: @dancelegz

# "If You Stumble, Remember to Make it a Part of the Dance."

So I made it? Welcome to the show! I'm your host for this portion of the book, and I go by the name of DanceLegz. However, I was born Denise Ella Wesley. My mother, a Chicago native and professional ballroom skater, gave me that name because of a good friend who just so happened to be a French woman. My middle name was doted upon me by my grandmother, and my last name is from my grandfather. I was born at Cook County Hospital around 3:50 p.m., during one of Chicago's worst snowstorms. It is said that my grandmother knew I was going to be a "mover and a shaker" like her, because of my constant persistence to push up on my legs at just two days old. The doctors and nurses would stop by and watch as I surely attempted to turn over or push up from my padding as if there was someplace better to be. I was first introduced to roller skating after discovering my mother's ice skates and roller shoe plates in a pantry closet at my grandmother's home. Without directions, my mother found me, then a seven-year-old, attempting to roller skate on a concrete slate in the backyard. It was not long before I was asking all types of questions about these magical wheels that strapped onto my little shoes. What were the odds? My mother had kept her performance skates after all these decades, hidden in a pantry. I was determined to make my mother teach me how to be just as amazing with these magical shoe skates.

I grew up as an only child with an imagination that stretched as far as can be. I was often found watching music videos and then attempting to copy the movements. My mother and grandmother would always catch little me standing in front of the TV or radio and doing whole

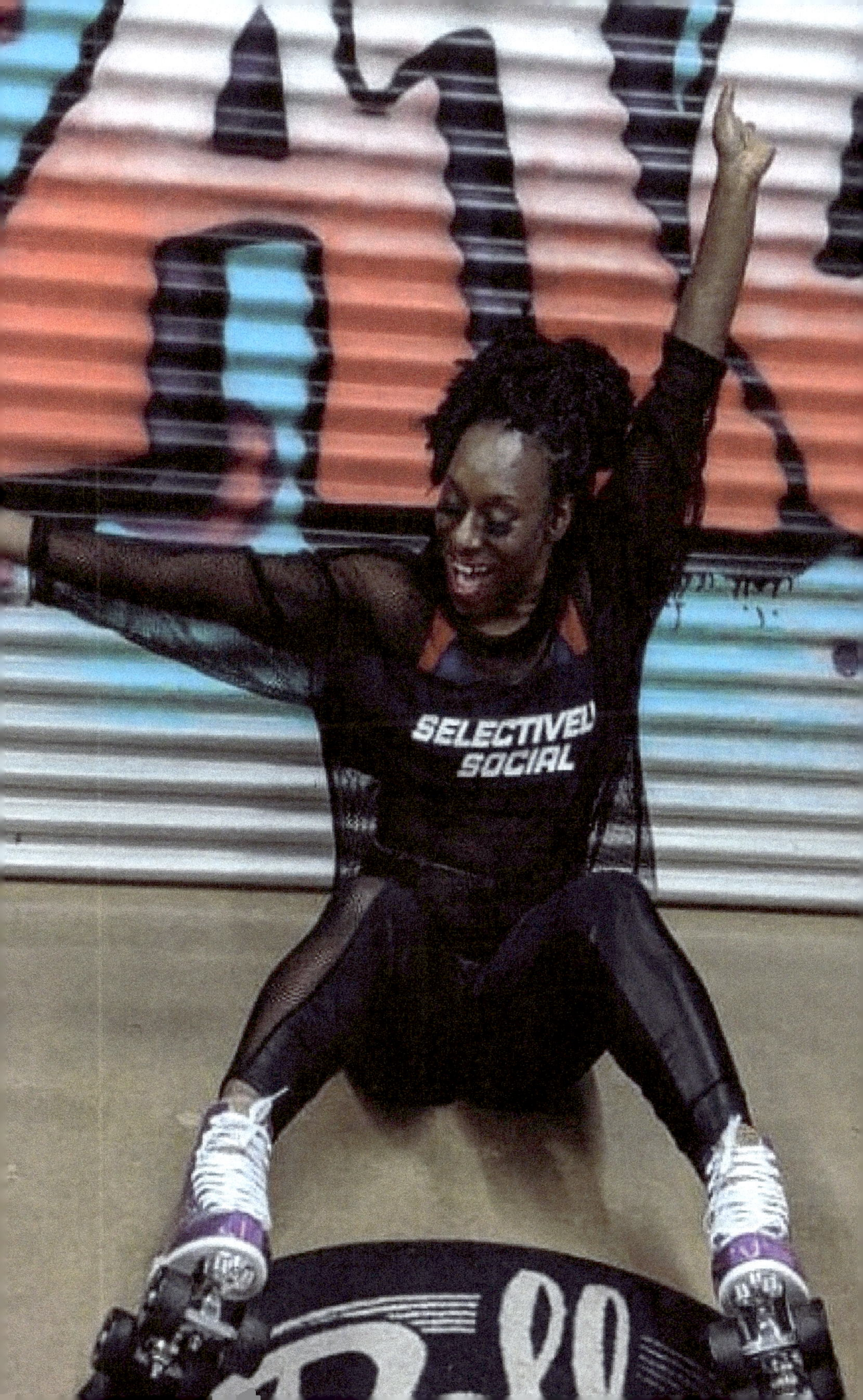
SELECTIVELY
SOCIAL

routines, almost to the exact rhythm as the music playing. At nine years old, I asked my mother for a skate party and, of course, a pair of my own skates. My mother would soon have a little skater on her hands, as I eventually attempted to skate in the house, on the porch, the front yard, backyard, up and down the sidewalk of our Englewood home…I made the world my skating rink. My mother decided to take me to a skating rink called Rainbo, located at the time on Clark Street (the North Side of Chicago) and it would be where I received my first pair of skate boots, "The Chicago Artistic." They were white, which at the time denoted "female" skates, and had bright pink wheels and laces. Although they were my first pair of skate boots, they would be the only time I would be seen in a plain white boot. I have skated in two pairs of dominions, one pair of combat boots (which I eventually had airbrushed), the Moxi Skate "purple molly," the "Glitter Glam" Crazy Skate (Australia) and my current indoor skate boot by Riedell. I needed a new pair of skate boots after one of my boots ripped and sparked the interest of a skate shop (Roll ATL) in Atlanta, Georgia. When asked why I needed several pairs of skate boots, I replied, "Photo shoots require a different skate boot sometimes, and Pole Skating (yes exactly as it sounds) requires a lighter boot than my roller skate rink boot. I noted (for example) "The Riedel skate boot is best suited for indoor skate sessions at the local rinks, as it provides the best ankle support for my routines." Okay, guess it is safe to say I have earned the name "DanceLegz" by default.

Roller skating is not just a sport for me, it is my life. I often say, "Don't invite me if my skates can't come, too." Apparently, while serving in the United States Navy, I was stopped in the hallway of the ship for roller skating. I was eventually entered into an event called "Saturday Night Live at The Bataan" where it was discovered that I could dance. I would become a regular and form a group with a few other sailors known as "The Navy's Divas." Oddly enough, I do not seem to be smitten by large crowds, but appear to be quite comfortable. I become DanceLegz or DanceLegz becomes me…the verdict is still out on this one (laughs). I wondered if I'm driven by any force or goal, however, I state that I live by one set of morals. "Always know what you WILL and WON'T do for money… ALL money IS NOT good money."

I merely want to earn a decent living and leave this Earth better than I came into it. I state that money is merely a tool used to access certain people and places. "Sometimes it allows you to appear like you belong..." I say, but in the end, it is what you can do, and how you treat people that get you to certain levels. I state that many opportunities have been turned down because the money was just not worth my morals. So why keep roller skating? What do I get out of it? Do I ever get bored? I hold on to the love I had when I was little, as well as all the places that roller skating has taken me. I state that roller skating literally saved my life at one point, after the passing of my mother and exit from the military. I would drive my car to rink after rink during the week just to roller skate, it gave me exercise, movement, purpose, and forced me to not mentally check out. 2010 to 2013 was rough for me, however, it allowed me to be around people at a time where, I state, was quite touch and go. I admit that so many skaters are alive today because of roller skating, be it the rinks, the skate parties, or simply being out of the trouble. "It is difficult to get into trouble when learning how to do a low shuffle or a 360-spin into a stride." Okay, so "DanceLegz" speaks skate lingo too from time to time. So what does roller skating even mean to me? I admit that there are plenty of sports and hobbies that could keep my interest, however, roller skating is like dancing on wheels, and what better way to live life than in motion? I attribute my bouts with depression and making it out to moments when I would simply roller skate to music in my living room. I did this for weeks until I say God gave me a notion that what I had to do was bigger than my living room. I state that then was when my look on life completely changed.

I am full of laughter and funny stories; I keep the humor going almost instantly. I shared with us the fact that I hope to one day become a guest on NBC's Saturday Night Live tv show. I promise to keep my roller skates in my suitcase until filming is over. (We find this hard to believe) DanceLegz can be found giving roller skating instructions, offering movement therapy to my clients, choreography for several people, and using my background in psychology and human resources as a consultant. I am the CEO and owner of DEW Vision, LLC and currently reside in Atlanta, Georgia. At thirty-eight, I show no signs of slowing down and say that I am still learning so much about the industry of roller skating, dance, and the history behind them both. I state that there is a lot of ridicule about if skaters should be dancing, or if dancers should be skating…however, I state that for me, the two go hand in hand and have created the brand that surrounds "DanceLegz". I admit that the skate world is not nearly as large as some might think and that there is a bond that most roller skaters have, which is, at times, more so felt than spoken about. The energy that comes from the skate floor during a roller skate session is absolutely life-changing, and once you are hooked, I doubt that it ever fades. Although my mother and grandmother have since passed, I believe that giving the freedom to roller skate to so many people is purposeful and accessible at any age. Keeping rinks open should remain at the forefront for all communities. They keep the body in motion, provide a space of belonging, joy, love, and even relaxation for so many people. However, without skaters and even non-skaters support, roller rinks will continue to go out of business. "We must continue to attend sessions and take our children, nieces, nephews, and godchildren…" I say.

Over the years I have seen roller skating in arenas that could have only been dreamed of when my mother was a performer. However, quads and roller blades appear seamlessly all over the world, and in so many industries. I give a small smile and say that I could have never imagined all the places my eight wheels have been and remain excited about the many opportunities that may be granted moving forward. I think back to all the people who told me to stop skating so much, stop dancing and just skate, or proclaimed that I needed to "grow up" and find other things to do with my time. With the tears that fell, I say I wished my mom and grandmother could see where those rusted roller skates took me, and that I make my ancestors proud. It was at that moment Denise and DanceLegz became one person, one identity. The skater and the dancer accepted that roller skating was more than a hobby or something to pass the time, but a source of life, love, joy, and happiness.

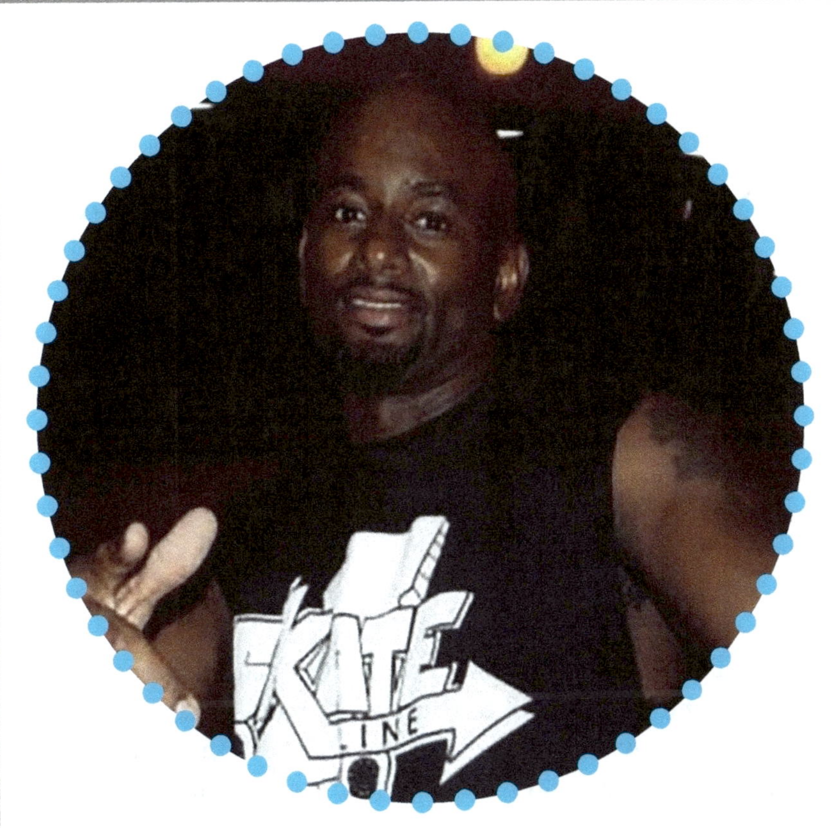


# Odis Rowlett

## aka O.D.

Facebook: @Odis Rowlett | Instagram: @dallas_sk8fairclassic

# "The Original SKATE-A-HOLIC"

That's what he's most known for when it comes to the Texas Sk8 Fair Classic. A skate Jam I created that technically was not even supposed to be a national skate party.

Born and raised in Longview, Texas, where roller skating as a kid was always the Friday night hype.

Little did I know that in 2007 I would revisit my childhood pastime as an adult and literally did not fit into the adult skate scene. I was horrible. For a guy like me, coming from East Texas and moving to Dallas, it was a faster and different environment. However, over the years, I've quickly acclimated into a lil' city, country boy. After attending a kid's skate party, I thought I was ready to start back skating again because I had a few skills from my childhood. So, a friend of mine invited me to Southern Skates on the Southside of Dallas. That's where all the magic began. However, that's where I realized these house skates weren't going to cut it if I planned to keep up with these cats. At that time, the Southside Boys and Showtime Rollers were the premier skate groups. People laughed at me and labeled me as that guy who would "just be in the way." I was told, "Man, get you some real skates if you plan on being an avid skater." I said to myself, "When I get this, I'm gon' be cold-blooded."

I took that advice and bought skates from another rink in Grand Prairie called Forum Roller World. I was on my way, at least I thought. Then came the real task of keeping up and learning.

Lucky for me, several other skaters were in my beginning class of new skaters. I literally skated four to five times a week, honing my skate

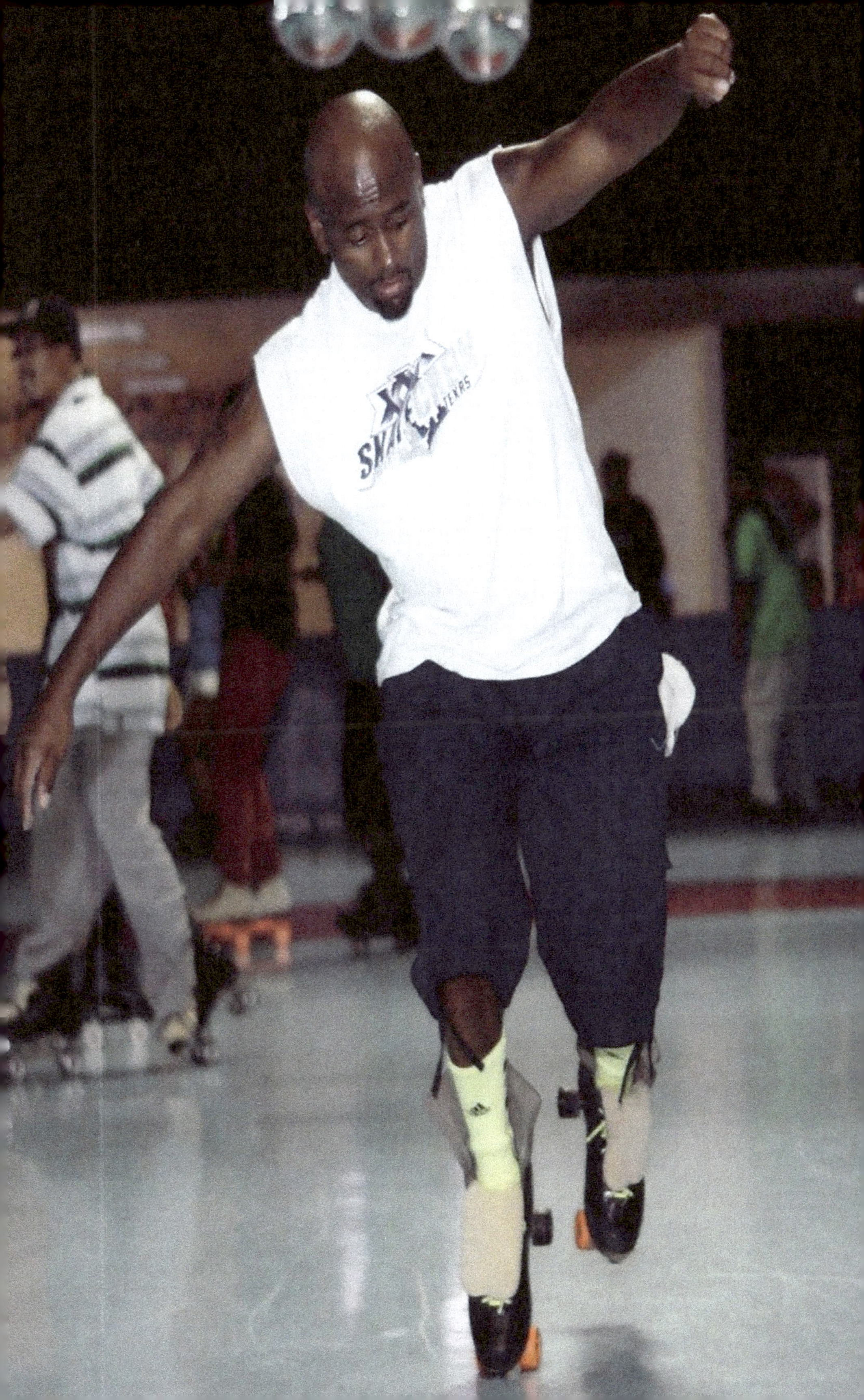

skills. Needless to say, I ran through three pairs of Riedell skates in three years. That's when I knew it was time to purchase the infamous O.G. Skates. I wanted that style with the fur on the tongue hanging down. As soon as I put my foot in that boot and hit the floor, In my mind, a star was born.

Roller skating became a great source of cardio and a great hobby while meeting good people along the way. Then came being part of a skate club. Always fun and challenging at the same time. Then I heard some of the seasoned skaters start talking about going out of town to skate. I was like, "What's wrong with just skating right here?" They replied, "It's a whole other level." So, me and my crew were like, "Yes let's do it," thinking we were about to go out of town and straight show our asses.

Memphis, Tennessee, with the Rolling Wheels of Memphis, was my very first out-of-town skate party, outside of the Texas Skate Jam with Black and the Showtime Rollers here in Dallas.

When I got to Memphis…let me tell y'all, we could not even get on the floor they were skating so fast, and it seemed like there were three thousand very skilled skaters on the floor going one hundred miles per hour.

Remember, we were all new skaters so we didn't have skills on the outside. We mostly did our line steps on the inside. So that was my safe zone—the middle. I quickly realized what the DJ was referring to when he announced, "Slower skaters on the inside and faster skaters on the outside." Basically, get your ass out of the way, like TI's crew said in the movie *ATL*. I then knew that adult Style skating was serious and no joke. I left Memphis rejuvenated and had new motivation to skate more.

After returning to Dallas, my ears had been hypnotized by what we now call skate music. That national sound just hit differently. So, for any new skaters reading this, just know pre-pandemic and before roller skating started a new trend after COVID, we were already doing what you guys and many others have gravitated to, but we're glad to have you all carry on and add to the culture.

One of the skate organizations I was a part of decided my skate name should be the name of our crew. So, I was forced to pick a new one. Anyone who knows me can tell you I'm Mr. Overkill. I had like three skate names. I was One Sleeve because I would cut one of my sleeves off my skate shirts. Then I was Krazzy Legzz because it was literally the hardest skate move for me to learn and master. I then I named myself Idle Wild because anyone who was following me in a routine or skate move, know I would literally start doing something else without notice. I just refused to be called ADD, so Idlewild fit better. I got the name from the movie Outkast made.

Fast forward to the aftermath of humble skate beginnings and many life changes that help you learn and grow. I started the Texas Sk8 Fair Classic as a four-hour skate party. This was a party just to have after we went to the fair in Dallas. The end of September and the beginning of October was always the Grambling and Prairie View football game and the battle of the bands at the fairgrounds. The name came from my rendition of the Texas State Fair Classic, but don't y'all tell nobody, okay? At that time, quite a few skaters came from near and far, so I figured, let's have a little skate party. Nothing major just us skating after the fair. The club scene was getting played out and the afterparties always ended with fights or shooting. The rink was a safer place to be. There were a lot of people that were pessimistic that it wouldn't be a good turnout, but hey, when you have a vision you can't listen to the doubters. You just have to move forward. The first year was a hit. We had 78 people. Sounds funny, but I really didn't expect that many. Soon after, more people came from Houston, Oklahoma, and Louisiana. It was a regional party. With me skating so much around the country, networking with other skaters, and attending out-of-state skate parties, other skaters saw the party and wanted to come. Most skate parties are two or three days or more.

I added some upcoming DJs to the line-up as well as some local DJs. After consulting with some of the more seasoned Icons in the skate world, I decided to go more regional/semi-national and made a *big mistake*. I reached out to DJ Joe Bowen who I didn't realize was on the Queen City Rollerz skate jam. I felt so bad; I totally canceled the whole idea. Nobody told me to check Skate Groove to see if any other parties were already on the same weekend. This was when people actually respected *not* having skate jams the same weekend or even close to a well-established party. *The idea of the classic was obliterated.* Then almost immediately Joe called me back and said, "Hey, they actually took me off the party. I'm available if you still want to do it." Feeling uneasy about it, and after we talked about it further, we decided to proceed.

Both of our states had long-running national parties with Rolling in The Carolinas and the Texas Skate Jam. We concluded that two regional parties could probably coexist with respect. Technically speaking, we were both planning skate parties without knowing at the same time. Also because of reasons I'll never say, The Classic was supposed to come out in 2010 but got delayed until 2011. That's why you have to keep your ideas and vision to yourself until it's time to set things in motion. I eventually reached out to the coordinators that I knew from the other party and we pretty much had mutual respect for one another, and I always promoted both parties. My skate travels have taken me from Texas to Atlanta, Chicago, Huntsville, Tennessee, California, Louisiana, Oklahoma, Arkansas, and Baltimore, and I even got nominated for an Adrenalin Award. I haven't been to all the skate parties, but eventually, I will. I've performed with SkateAHolics and Triple Skate Crew on many occasions, as well as with some individual skaters. I'm truly honored to be a part of such a great anthology of skaters and their stories. This book is such an opportunity for us as skaters to tell our stories, as well as explain how we've cultivated our skate lives along the way. And that this book is coming out in 2021 after the pandemic canceled so many skate parties. The 10th Annual Texas Sk8 Fair Classic has just gotten a lot better. I can't express how many people and friends have supported and helped over the years. ***I just want to say thank you all.*** Having the overall support of skaters nationally and internationally; we have seen our numbers grow astronomically over the years from just under one hundred people to more than five hundred at the main event.

As of today, I still enjoy roller skating and all that it has to offer, although I'm more on the business and coordinating side of things now. I can't wait to get back to traveling out of town to skate jams again. One thing that I really enjoy the most about being at the rink is new skaters. To pass my skills and knowledge on to any new skater, DJ, or future coordinator and see them succeed brings me pleasure. It has been a wonderful journey, learning all the behind-the-scenes hard work of putting on skate parties. Even to the point of doing one-day parties like the first R&B Skate Party ever in Dallas that I had and was a huge success. And to think I actually tried to retire in 2019. However, after all the skaters that patronize The Classic who poured out their love for the event and the popular demand for it, I can honestly say, like Bee1ne said, "This is a good party for the culture."

In conclusion, I thank God for this journey. I stay humble and remember that it's for the ***SKATERS ALWAYS***.

## Do You Know...

### Neon Lights and Decor

Roller skating rinks of the mid-20th century were known for their vibrant and visually stimulating environments, characterized by neon lights and colorful decorations. Neon lights adorned the walls and ceilings of the rinks, casting a radiant glow that illuminated the skating area and created an atmosphere of excitement and energy. The neon lights, often in bright and eye-catching colors, captivated the attention of skaters and added to the overall ambiance of the rink.

In addition to neon lights, roller skating rinks featured a variety of decorations designed to enhance the skating experience. Mirrored balls suspended from the ceiling reflected the neon lights, creating dazzling patterns of light that danced across the walls and floor of the rink. Disco balls, another popular decor element, added to the disco-era aesthetic of roller skating rinks, casting shimmering reflections that intensified the festive atmosphere.

The combination of neon lights and colorful decorations transformed roller skating rinks into lively and immersive spaces where skaters could escape into a world of fun and excitement. The visually stimulating environment heightened the sensory experience of roller skating, captivating the imaginations of skaters and spectators alike. Roller skating rinks became iconic symbols of leisure and recreation, beloved by generations of individuals who embraced the vibrant culture of roller skating during its heyday in the mid-20th century.

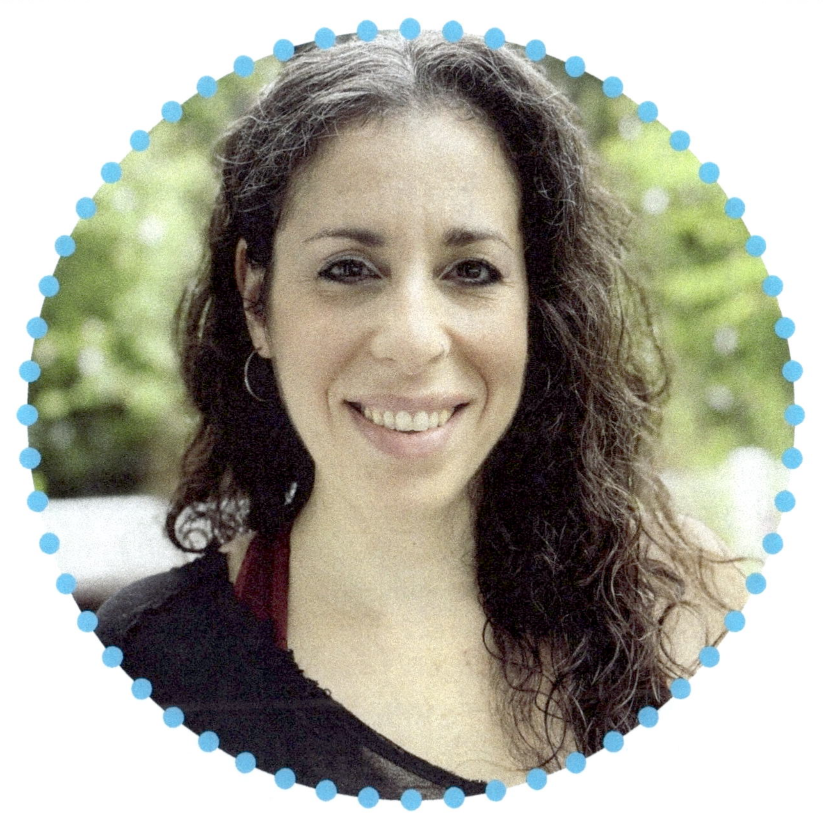

# Jaclyn Duncan

Facebook: @Jaclyn Duncan | Instagram: @rollingintune

## "Hard work beats talent when talent doesn't work hard."

Almost every human has a few distinct early childhood memories. They're usually pivotal, often emotionally charged, and generally fewer in number than we have fingers. One of my clearest memories from that time in my life was being just a few feet off the ground, wheels on my feet, rolling around a shiny-floored school gymnasium. I couldn't have been more than four years old.

I learned years later that my mother had enrolled me in a weekly skate class for toddlers. And this is where my roller skating journey begins.

My grandmother was a skater in the 1940s in North Jersey. Perhaps because of this, my childhood garage was always stocked with skates in my size. I more recently learned that a great aunt on the other side of my family was a skater, too. So maybe I was destined to skate? After all, it's in my blood! Growing up, I spent countless hours skating in my driveway with my sister. I can't remember not loving it. Thanks to the wonders of VHS technology, she and I would record ice skating competitions that were played on repeat and carefully studied. We would then go out to our garage, lace-up, and attempt to mimic what we saw on the screen. We must have watched the '88 Olympics women's long program at least one hundred times. I was ten, she was six. That's how I learned to do front and back crossovers, a spread eagle, and a basic spin. I think I even managed a three-turn along the way!

For a brief stint between seventh grade and my sophomore year in high school, there was a rink in the next town over. The floor wasn't wood, and it catered to us teens. I remember being one of the better

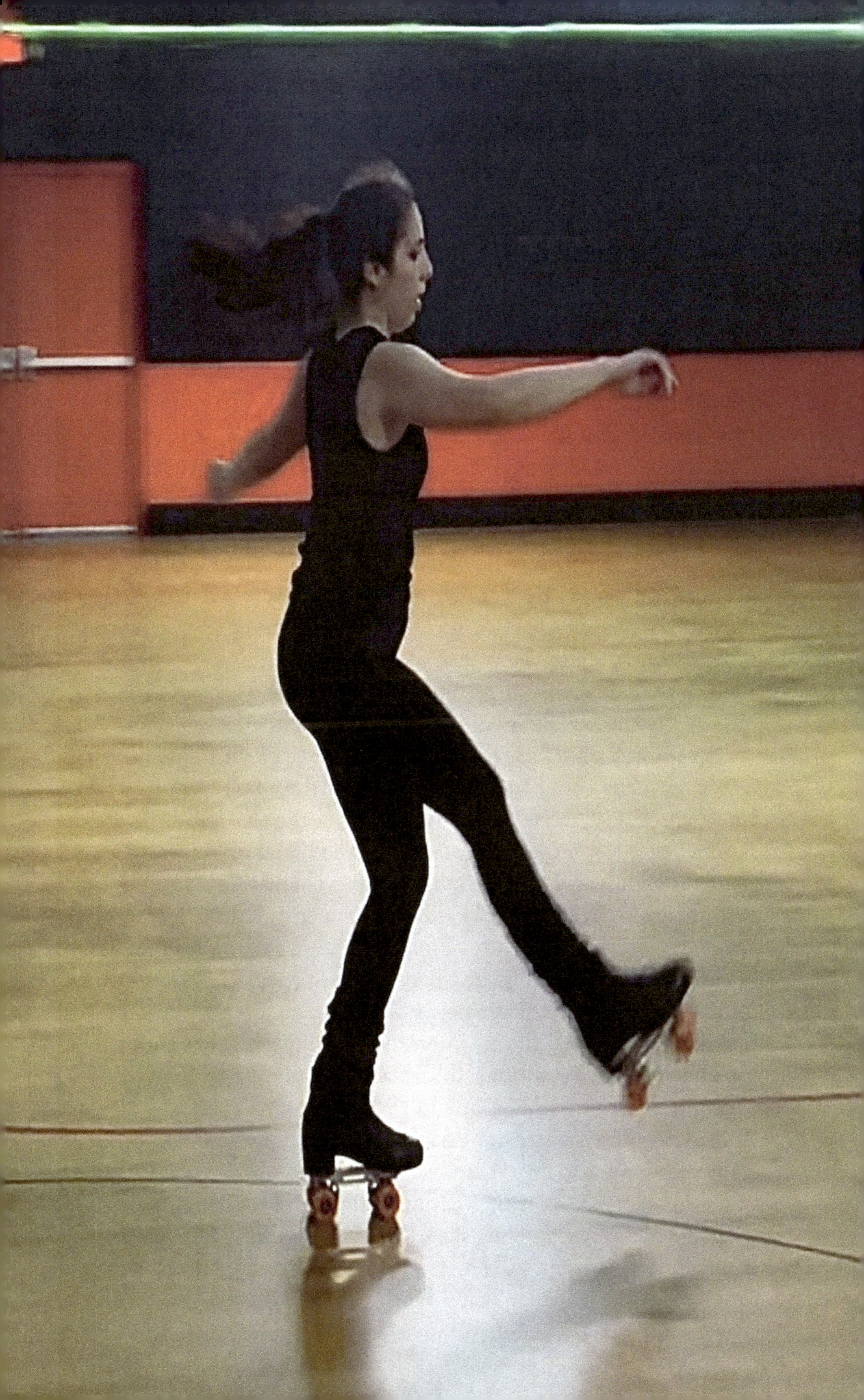

skaters there besides the staff, whose feet I'd stare at, trying to decipher their footwork. In the roughly twenty times I went to that rink for 4 years, the floor guards' grooves were my sole exposure to any form of rhythm/dance skating until 2018.

High school came and so did inline skating. My original Rollerblade brand skates and wrist guards quickly became a cherished item! They were my second major purchase following my skis. They got carried off to university in Boston with me and were dusted off a couple of times each semester through my college years. If you know Boston, you know the Esplanade: a long flat bike trail along the Charles River containing the outdoor concert venue, the Hatch Shell. From 1996 to 2000, every weekend, inline skaters would set up lines of cones at the Hatch Shell. The most skilled skaters slalomed through with the most impressive footwork on wheels I'd ever seen. Though my blades weren't set up for those sorts of tricks, I was inspired and would try it anyway, even if I made it through just two cones!

Then life happened. I graduated from school. I moved to Tokyo. I returned to the US and in 2004 I became a mother.

As a lover of travel, for years I was part of an online network where travelers could find hosts while on the road, completely free. I participated in the community as both a traveler and host. In the summer of 2017, a German woman by the name of Vera Englehardt came through New Jersey on her way cross-country. As a lover of roller skating, she had a dream to "skate across America." She'd flown to New York City and was headed for Philadelphia—I was on her way. Before her arrival, she'd explained her plans for her trip and I shared with her my childhood love for skating—I hadn't skated more than five times in roughly fifteen years, but my interests were piqued by her enthusiasm! Vera had me digging my old Rollerblades out of my basement to go for a spin in a nearby parking lot and all I could do was smile! Later, she let me try on her quads, and I guess you can say, the rest was history. I really didn't want to give them back.

In February 2018, while visiting a friend in Florida, I discovered a shop in Miami Beach selling skates and purchased my first set of quads as an adult. I returned to New Jersey, where the weather was too cold to skate outside. My new skates sat by the back door.

2018 wasn't an easy year for me. At all. A dear friend took their own life that May, throwing me into a sea of grief. I cried daily while running through the same stories in my head on repeat. In mid-August, my head popped above water long enough to notice my unused roller skates. I started Googling local rinks. I snapped a photo of my skates to drop on Facebook, asking if any friends wanted to join me, but not a single person bit. So, on Tuesday, August 26, 2018, at a tender forty years old, I arrived solo at the doors of Holiday Skating Center (now The Rink) for their weekly adult session, featuring live organ music.

Wait. Rewind. Live organ music? Did I read that correctly?

Let me just say that skating to live organ music was *not* the typical entry point for most new skaters in 2018! I'm a musician. It's what I do for a living. When I saw "Live Organist" listed on Holiday's website, I *had* to see what it was all about! What I witnessed was nothing short of amazing and far beyond anything I could have imagined. Skaters from age twenty through their eighties, many in coordinated costumes with their partners, were shuffling, waltzing, and fox-trotting, with flawless footwork as they moved to the organ's beat. Solo skaters were working on figures at the rink's center while older, retired skaters sat on the benches, chatting with old friends. This wasn't a bunch of strangers. This was a community. I'd never seen anything like it. It was like I stepped back in time to the forties or fifties when my grandmother was a skater, but it was 2018! I knew I'd be back the following week.

As with any community, if you stick around long enough, you're bound to become part of it. Within a few months, I'd become friends with several other new skaters and started a group chat on Facebook Messenger which eventually grew to some fifty people before I moved it over to a Facebook group—Skate Skate Skate NJ!, a forum that has grown to roughly seven hundred New Jersey skaters to ask questions, share upcoming skate events, find a skate buddy, and more. Also, with each passing month, the healing salve of roller skating washed away the acute phases of my grief. As many will attest to, skating has an amazing ability to pull you out of your head and into the present moment. It was exactly what I needed at exactly the right time.

As my skate social circle grew, so did my curiosity about other rinks. I was also becoming exposed to multiple skate styles, though at this point I'd only really witnessed artistic skating, shuffling, and a little bit of rhythm/step routines. One day, just a couple of months into my skate journey, one of my first skate friends, John, asked, "So I can't really peg you. What kind of skater will you become? A shuffler? An artistic skater?" My reply was simply, "I want to do it all." Why not?

In October 2018, I was invited to attend a 1st Friday Advanced Skate session at Sk8 47 in Franklinville, New Jersey. It was there that I first saw Shamar Cunningham skate. He was effortlessly gliding across the floor, spinning on one foot while simultaneously bouncing to the music. He had such control and grace. I was instantly fascinated and incredibly inspired! I found John and pointed at Shamar. "*That. That* is what I want to do."

*Side note:* A quick shout-out to Shamar! For much of the latter half of 2019, Shamar became a real mentor to me, teaching me footwork, boosting my confidence to twist and turn at speed, and skating partners/trains with me. Without the time he invested in my skating, I'm not sure I'd have learned as quickly as I did. His contributions to my growth as a skater will forever remain a part of my skate story!

It was also around that time that I remember reaching down to my thigh to scratch a bug bite and discovering muscle! Wait, when did that get there? I was graduating from newbie to "skater" and from that point forward, I never skated less than three times a week.

One Sunday in November 2018, I was in Delaware for a gig. My skates were in my car and I got the itch, so I Googled around to see if there was a rink I could hit on the ride back to New Jersey. What popped up was Soul Night at Sk8 47. I was already familiar with that rink from the First Friday I'd attended, so I decided to give it a shot. This night was a pivotal moment in my skate journey! Let me preface this by saying, we all know how racially divided rink culture is on the East Coast. Outdoors is a bit different, but indoors, there are sessions that cater to traditionally white styles of skating and other sessions that cater to traditionally black styles. Being white, most of my early exposure to rink skating was within the white community. This was my very first time attending a "Soul Night." First off, I was blown away by the level of talent. It wasn't just one superstar skater, it was a whole rink full of skills! But more importantly, what really struck me was the shameless passion these skaters had for their craft. The energy, creativity, the joy, but most strikingly, the freedom of expression. This was a lifestyle for these people, and I wanted to know all about it. I dove in headfirst, and Sunday Soul Night became part of my weekly routine.

Come January 2019, I found myself planning a road trip cross country—it was something I'd always wanted to do, and I had some work out in Los Angeles. Plus, what better way to experience the depth and history of my newfound passion than to visit rinks along the way? Five months into my skate journey, my wheels rolled across floors in Richmond, Nashville, Oklahoma City, Denver, Las Vegas, Los Angeles, and San Diego. The education I received on that trip is beyond words. I witnessed regional styles and met countless skaters who welcomed me and were eager to share their knowledge. I skated my first skate park, saw "dipping" for the first time, learned to do the "downtown", was invited to skate with a partner, and got to skate the iconic Venice Beach. Most skaters aren't blessed with such an experience so early in their journey, and for this opportunity, I feel grateful. I returned to New Jersey with the beginnings of my own flow, birthed largely from the influences of the countless skaters I met along the way. From then on, a mindset I've had for years about travel was taken into my skate life: The best education comes when you leave the familiar behind. And in the case of skating, the gems you'll return home with are priceless. From it will emerge a style unique to YOU!

When I got back from my cross-country trip, I went *hard*. Millennium Skate World in Camden, New Jersey, where I dug deep into rhythm skating, became a second home and my Saturday nights were spent at Rollerjam USA in Staten Island, New York, where I grew passionate about learning to skate with a partner. Skating solo is great, but skating with a partner really tickled the musician in me. It was like jamming with a band! I loved how much it relied on good reaction time and thinking on your toes—exactly the space I thrive in musically. It's not unlike the feeling I get in the studio if I'm asked to improvise a solo over a track I'd never heard before. Once you develop sufficient technique, even though you may not know what's coming, you can trust that your skills and intuition will carry you! What a rush! Beats pumping, your partner's hand in yours while you bounce in unison, sweat pouring off your brow and dripping to the floor. Rollerjam was a vibe, and I was hooked.

One night around that time, I looked at my skates and nearly broke into tears. It was like they were a part of me all along. A skill laying dormant under the surface since childhood was finally being tapped. I had never been an athlete before. Music was my primary focus throughout much of my life, leaving no room for sports. Plus, I'd always been a horrible runner. I dismissed athletics as "not being for me" very early on. But as I picked up my skates and held them in front of me, all I could feel was that I was made for this. How these strange boots on wheels had changed my life already, and I'd been skating for less than nine months.

That spring, I got the wild idea to combine my skills as a musician with roller skating and filmed the world's first flute and cello duo on roller skates. The video became a bit of a YouTube/Facebook sensation within the skate community, and, "Wait, are you the flute player?" became a common question for me to hear at rinks! Come summer, I'd added Central Park in New York City and Branch Brook Park in Newark, New Jersey, to my list of favorite places to skate and by January 2020, I'd attended my first national skate party (Tampa Soul Roll).

Midway through the throes of the 2020 quarantine, I decided to dedicate my YouTube channel (which was previously just music) to skating. At first, I posted just my own skate videos but later, as rinks began to open again, I shifted to filming notable skate sessions and parties, as well as providing gear reviews (I'm a geek!) and tutorials. My purpose, largely being to introduce the new wave of 2020/2021 skaters to what roller skating has to offer as a *culture*. Skating is *not* just the dance moves seen in isolation on TikTok! And more specifically, as a white skater, I sought to expose other non-black skaters to the depth and beauty of black roller skating in America. Until 2018, I knew none of this existed. To me, roller skating was just an outdoor activity or something kids did at birthday parties, as is the case for many white Americans. Now that people of all races, cultures, and backgrounds are lacing up, my desire is to see the trending skate styles, which originated in black America, not just be mimicked from afar, but to be experienced up close and to be understood from the root. What better way to introduce this rich history to the world than sharing through my own eyes, this beautiful culture that I've grown to not just love, but be a part of?

As I filmed session after session, party after party, it really struck me how none of the absolutely incredible feats we achieve on that wood floor have a rule book. These styles and techniques have been organically passed down from generation to generation, OG to beginner, mentor to student. How much in this modern age is left where we can say this? In the coming decades, it won't surprise me if techniques are formally established and taught with parameters, as is the case with most sports. What a special time to be alive and roller skating, and to be a part of that organic process! There's magic in knowing that the footwork you do today was carried for decades through countless skaters before reaching *you*. I urge all skaters to not forget that.

Now, in August 2021, just three full years into my skate journey and only a full year into posting skate content on YouTube, I've come to realize that my reach and influence have gone far beyond what I could have imagined. I've been approached at rinks near and far by skaters of all backgrounds, thanking me for answering their questions about gear and techniques. But one of the most special moments was just a few weeks ago when an older gentleman recognized me, introduced himself, and credited my session videos for helping him stay positive through quarantine. I was at a loss for words! At that moment, I realized that what I do is so much bigger than me. I feel honored to accept that torch and will carry it proudly.

I'll close by saying skating wasn't something that came on slowly for me. I had no idea how my life would change when I stepped into that rink in August 2018. In a strange way, I'd say, I didn't find skating, skating found me. Maybe that's the way it is for those of us who fall in love with it. Was that early childhood memory in the gymnasium foreshadowing this moment? All I know is that I'm beyond thankful to have found such joy and that I will continue to lace up within the community until my feet will no longer carry me!

# Do You Know...

## Roller Skating and Organ Music

Roller skating rinks of the mid-20th century were known for their vibrant atmosphere, with live organ music being a central element of the experience. Skaters would glide across the rink to the lively tunes played on pipe organs or electronic keyboards, creating a festive ambiance. The organ music provided a rhythmic backdrop for skaters, enhancing their enjoyment of the activity and adding to the overall excitement of the rink.

Many roller skating rinks featured skilled organists who entertained patrons with a diverse repertoire of music, ranging from upbeat melodies to familiar tunes that encouraged skaters to dance and move with the rhythm. The live music added a personal touch to the roller skating experience, creating a sense of connection between the organist and the skaters. The organist's ability to adapt the music to the energy of the crowd helped to maintain the lively atmosphere of the rink throughout the skating session.

The combination of organ music, neon lights, and colorful decorations contributed to the unique charm of roller skating rinks during this era. Skaters of all ages enjoyed the immersive experience of gliding across the rink while being serenaded by the melodic tunes of the organ. The live music became synonymous with the roller skating culture of the time, evoking fond memories for those who frequented the rinks and contributing to the nostalgic appeal of roller skating today.

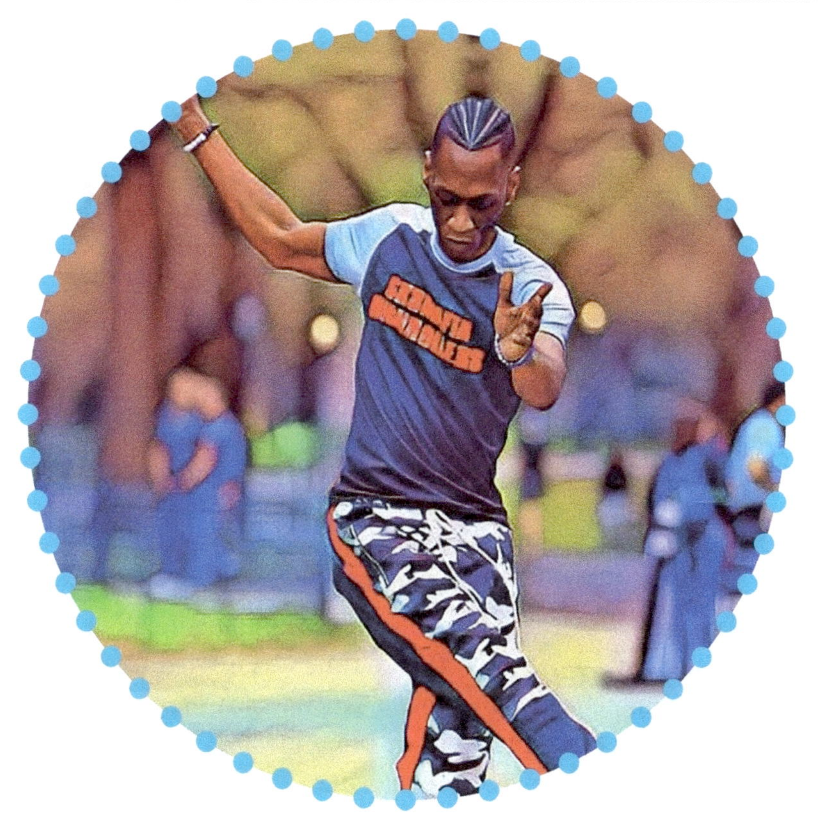

Lionel Laurent

Facebook: @Lionel Laurent | Instagram: @sk8mafiahighrollers

# "SKA8MAFIA HIGHROLLERS"

Inner-city kids in New York City. What we did for fun was roller skate. Your mother gave you $10. Skating cost $5 and the other five hit the Chinese spot, order chicken wings and French fries—it was a great day. We had a space to hang out with no parents; we're chilling like we were grown. Meanwhile, politics was building up around us but we were young, living life in N.Y.C.  Crime was high, drug use was on the rise. The climate was changing. Ed Koch wasn't the greatest mayor, but his tenure had our city in a more prideful vibe.

The Dinkins era was a segway to the Giuliani era, which led to shutdowns of many dance venues. Times started changing as far as skating. My local roller rink was a roller disco. There was an adult night, which meant B.Y.O.B., on Tuesday night with Big Bob playing some house music remixes of Frankie Knuckles. Women got sexy and dressed to roller skate for the low price of $8. Skating was the date night go-to in the urban community, a sort of safe haven. Isolated incidents that occurred at our rink were from non-skaters, just troublemakers in the neighborhood who had nothing to do.  The rink closed because of corporate greed and our stupidity of not landmarking such a place. It's a storage facility now. The place that kept me off the streets is gone.

The nineties were not so good for me. I was a victim of a violent crime that left me stabbed eight times and angry. My relaxation and rehabilitation were from skating. My skate path started on the local rink floor.  Empire Roller Disco was iconic in many ways even ahead of its time.  Bill Butler, Vincent Smith, Lil Mike, Slo Mo, Boo to the classy

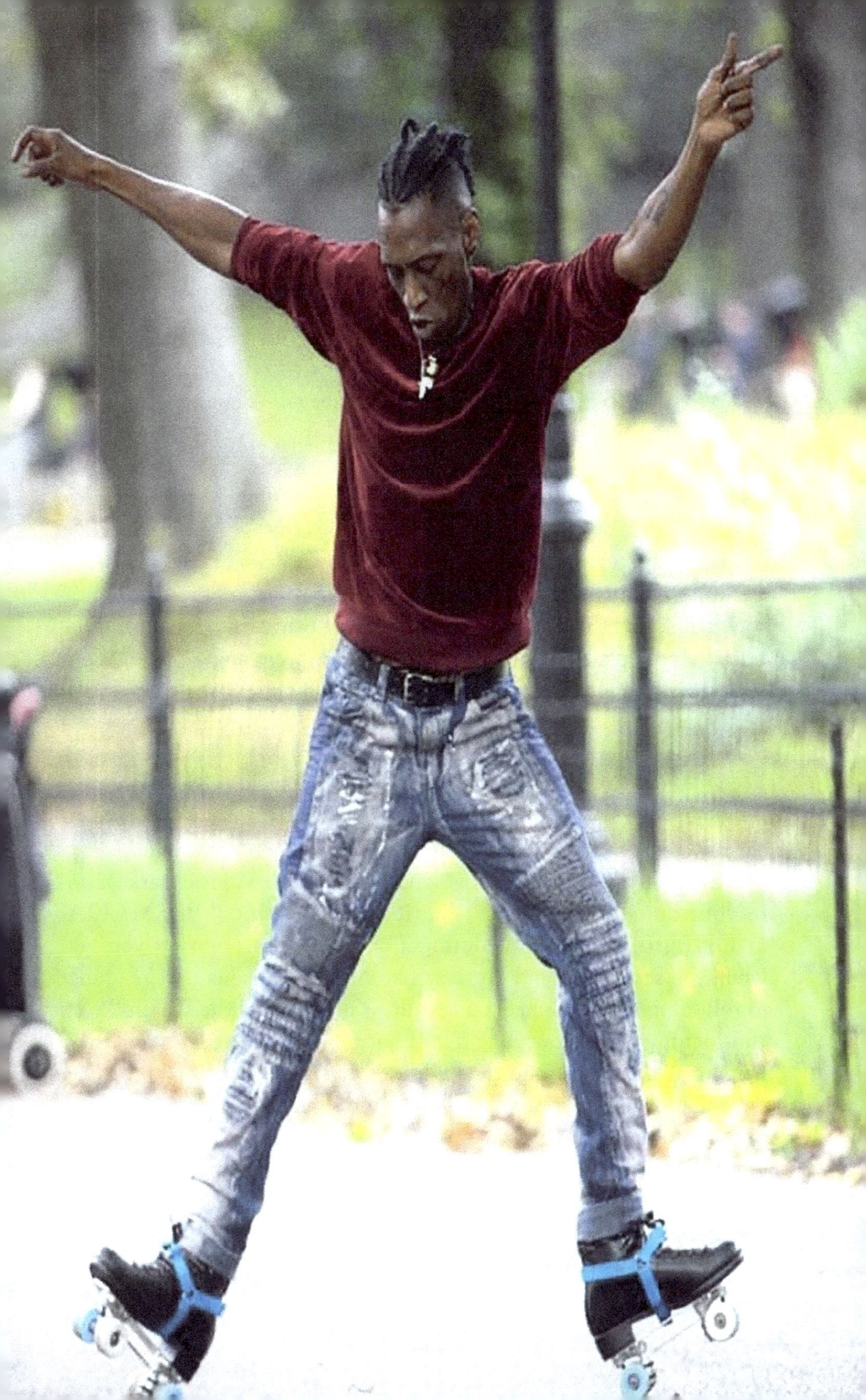

suits from Icefromphilly. In N.Y.C., we struggled to keep skating alive. Tanya Dean (skaterobics), Lyñna Davis, Bob Nichols (C.P.D.S.A), Harry Martin's (ROLLERWAVE) Chelle Pollard (skateinfonetwork) Amy Collado (Butter Roll) Bklyn Sk8s (Crummy) which was started by Skate legend Lezly Zerring. The dates I can't be exact on. That was a time in my life where things were moving fast and N.Y.C. was a party mecca.

We skated as kids and now use this to cope with depression, divorce, or any of the trials and tribulations we go through. We feel free when the right song comes on, reminisce when the right song is played, have special moves and routines which differs from state to state, rink to rink, which makes skating so unique from the Chicago JB to New York (househead) styles of skating. Each area has its moves and styles. As a culture, skating has always been around but never represented in a way that shows the lifestyle. TikTok did not bring back roller skating. Social media played a part of course, but we were always doing this. The sound of glorious music and beautiful women. Let's go skating. I skate because I feel free when I do it. The way the world is now, even the Sk8 world is monopolized.

Money and greed have changed many skaters and have created a different skate culture, but to deeply elaborate on that would take at least five books. Skating has turned into a lifestyle for many, including me. Skating has evolved from skating rinks to TV, local parks, and in your home again. In N.Y.C it's a family thing; SK8MAFIA HIGHROLLERS is the continuation of the skate feeling you get when you see your friends at the rink. My family is here, we're going to roll tonight. Ali Ishmael and Andre Villabrera are the skaters I can consider my brothers who help me continue our skate tradition. They help bring the energy and the night ends up a great night. Though we don't have many rinks, we push for the movement of roller skating and our style of it. I came from a music background and my sister used to bring music to the DJ so I got familiar with up-tempo skating and dancing. My brother took me skating to Park Circle Roller Rink in Park Slope in Brooklyn. The eye-opener: I saw guys battling, spinning, footwork, I was hooked. At the moment, the nicest rink I know of is Lakeside Prospect Park, which doesn't have an adult night. I wonder why? I know why; it's sad things haven't changed. Skating as a whole has evolved, but what can we or you do to preserve the culture?

My "EVOLUTION OF SKATING" might be a "REVOLUTION." Surround yourself with great people; make it an event. You meet so many wonderful people skating. If you see me, say "Hi." We are all skating and alive, we are not strangers. Rich or poor, Black or White on skates, we're skaters. We give free skate tutorials all over the city. If you're in New York, reach out. I consider all skaters family. I've achieved much success being a roller skater, but I don't talk much. I'm surprised I'm talking now. The opportunity to skate with so many different people and go many places... My advice to you: Get rollin'. It will change your life. It definitely kept me out of trouble.

# Do You Know...

## Rise in Popularity

Roller skating traces its origins back to the mid-1700s when Belgian musician John Joseph Merlin introduced the world's first roller skate with metal wheels. Merlin's invention, initially intended as a novelty device for entertainment, consisted of a pair of shoes with metal-wheeled plates attached to the bottom. These early roller skates lacked brakes and were difficult to maneuver, making them challenging to use.

Merlin's roller skates garnered attention for their novelty, but they did not immediately gain widespread popularity. It wasn't until later in the 18th century that roller skating began to attract interest, particularly as a recreational activity. Despite the initial challenges with Merlin's design, roller skating gradually evolved over the years, with improvements made to the skates' design and functionality.

The introduction of quad roller skates, featuring four wheels arranged in a square configuration, revolutionized the sport and paved the way for its widespread adoption. Quad skates provided greater stability and control, making roller skating more accessible to people of all skill levels. As roller skating continued to evolve, it became a beloved pastime and sport enjoyed by millions of people around the world.

Today, roller skating remains a popular activity, with enthusiasts participating in various forms of the sport, including recreational skating, roller derby, and artistic roller skating. While the early roller skates invented by John Joseph Merlin may have been rudimentary in design, they laid the foundation for a thriving and dynamic culture that continues to captivate people of all ages.

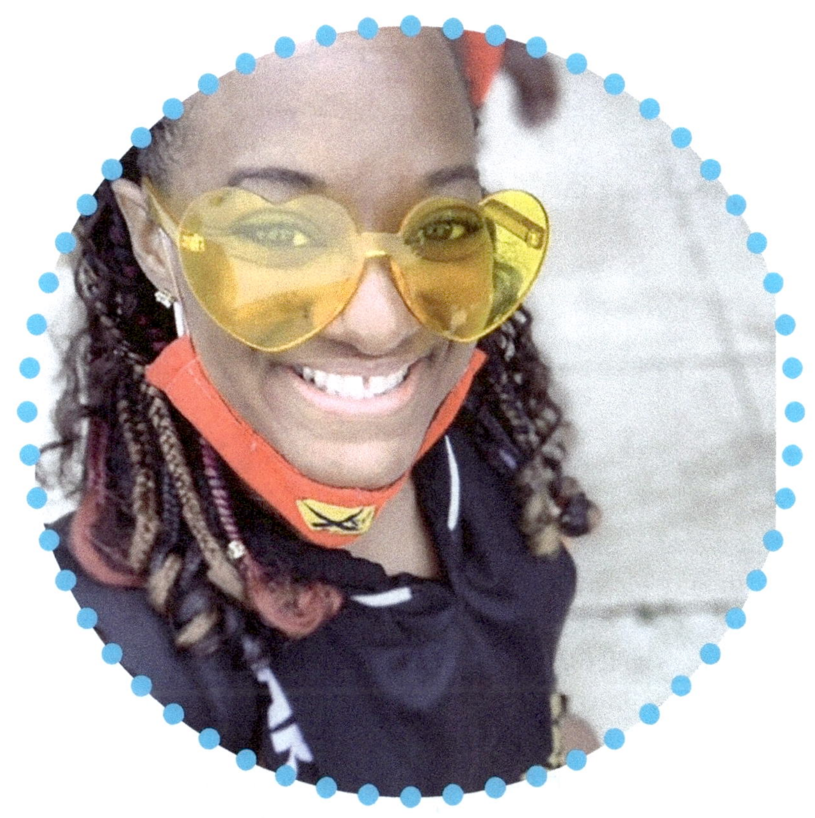

## Naimah Cyprian

### aka Xstra

Facebook: @Naimah “xstra” Cyprian | Instagram: @djxstra

# "My Skate Zone is Drama-free"

The evolution of skating for me began at seven years old when my sisters and I had to share a pair of roller skates. I don't remember who those skates belonged to, but I played in them a lot. They were too big for my feet, but I didn't care. Let me tell you, my single leg balance and core strength were definitely well developed. We took turns scooting. First the left boot and then the right, one boot at a time. Our mom eventually bought us each a pair—the colorful kind you clipped over your shoes.

We skated in the house across the wood floors from the living room's front window, through the dining room, and stopped at the kitchen's entrance. Growing up, we were the only kids with roller skates, while other kids had bikes, skateboards, scooters, or nothing else but just their sneakers. Skating outside was like an obstacle course, with rocks, cracks in the concrete, twigs, hills, and people grabbing to pull or spin on you around. Her two favorite outdoor places to skate were in the schoolyard's parking lot on the black tarp and inside the tennis court. I would roll outside until the sunset or dinnertime.

Also, at age seven, I started dance classes, tumbling, singing, playing piano, and playing numerous sports. When I became a teenager, around thirteen or fourteen, I started choreographing, performing, and creating performance music with a neighborhood dance troupe. During this time, I started traveling to local skating rinks for recreational skating. Having the chance to put on some real skates was like heaven. I had no problem seeking the best pair of brownies (rental skates). My nickname

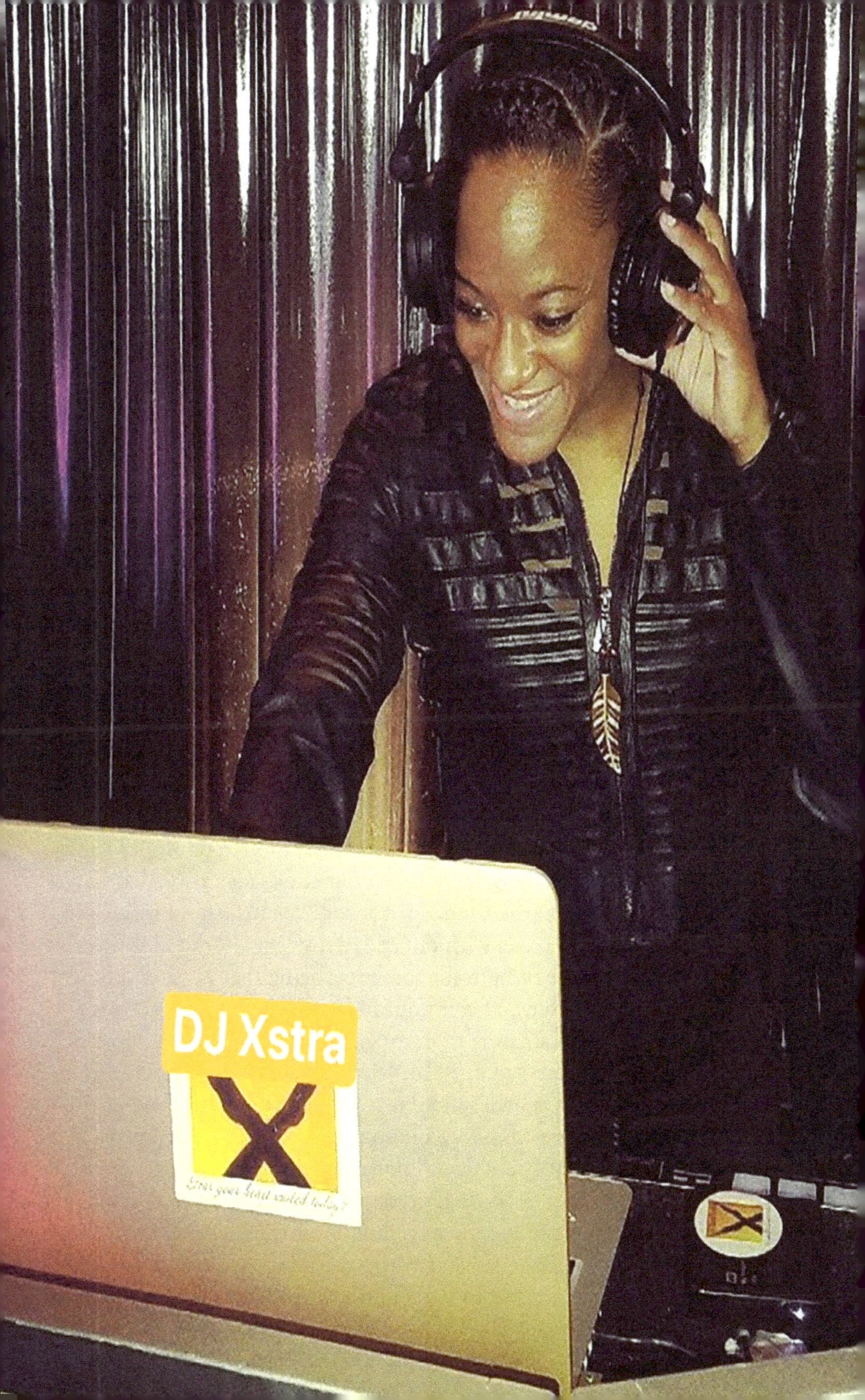
DJ Xstra
X

should've been "Lil Send Back." If I couldn't lace them up, if the wheels went left when I went right, if the toe stopper was loose, or I thought they looked bumpy and beat up, I would send them back for another pair.

I had a blast attending the family skate sessions, but I would *really* cut up at the teen sessions. My parents allowed me to go skating without them only if I was on a school field trip or going with a group of friends. Whenever I took public transportation with friends, and the sun had set before the session was over, I'd better be getting a car ride back home. Getting to the rinks I liked to attend, such as Route 66 on King Drive, The Rink on 87th, Rainbow Roller Rink up north, and Markham Roller Rink in the south suburbs, I had to travel miles away from my neighborhood. This meant I had to bypass many gang territories, which were no joke in the 1990s.

I really enjoyed traveling to various rinks within the Chicagoland area because I would see so many skate styles. It was a pleasing experience to meet new people from other communities, who also shared the same vibe and enjoyment I'd felt from going skating. This was about the actual time when I began taking skate trips. Like dancing, skating had allowed me to travel the world beyond the three-block radius of my home and from what I'd seen on television.

Most of the school's skate field trips were to Fleetwood Roller Rink near the west side or Olympic Fields Roller Rink (renamed Rich City Rink) in the south suburbs. Outside of school-related trips, I was really picky with whom I'd travel with outside of my neighborhood. I wasn't trying to fight anyone or fight for someone, being that far from home. I grew up in the Englewood community. For the record, not all blocks were or are dangerous. I was a pretty good kid growing up. Most of my friends parents used to say, "If Naimah isn't going, you can't go." My mom was a well-known school teacher and considered one of the 'neighborhood moms' within the community, so other parents knew she wasn't for any foolery. I sure would not risk being put on punishment.

Okay, here's a hidden truth. During my adolescent days, sometimes my sister closest to me in age, our childhood friends, and I used to sneak into the next skate session without paying. We would hide in the bathroom and come out to skate until we got caught, or just before the sun was setting. I was an adventurous and ambitious teenager, like most teens.

I found just as much satisfaction from going skating as I did attending house parties. In my teenage years, going to the teen skate sessions was everything! The rinks would use their smaller floor/practice area for dancing. OMG! The lights would be off and only the strobes lights would be on. It was juking. There was a separate DJ spinning party music, which differed from the main skate floor music. People who truly knew me from my neighborhood knew my first love was dancing and then I fell in love with skating. When the music would hit my soul, you could find me in the middle of every dance battle and freestyle circle. My crew would always hype me up to battle the best, especially the male dancers. This will always be my most memorable and favorite skate session because I could dance and then get my roll on. It was the best of both worlds in one night.

As I got older to get into the nightclubs, I would have a blast. However, everyone knew my first choice was to go skating, especially Saturday night's midnight rumble session—midnight to four o'clock in the morning. I loved the loud vibrational sound of the bass thumping through the speakers, how the DJs mixed the music, seeing people dance-skate, watching the skate crews do their routines, and having an unlimited opportunity to learn and practice new skate moves. My overall experience has always been welcoming within the skate and dance communities.

I feel absolutely free to express myself whenever I'm in my skates, wearing my kicks, or another pair of dance shoes. Escaping into my drama-free zone is my thing. It's in these avenues of performance arts, through dance, roller skating, and music where I find a source of energy to recharge. Roller skating is freedom for me. When I lace up, I'm clocking in to let loose in my drama-free zone, which is why I skate. Whatever is bothering me, I release that negative energy. This is my skate therapy. It's helped me keep my sanity while grieving the loss of my beloved grandparents and mom.

One time, a guy I dated, who was a non-skater, said, "So, you're going skating again?" He confessed he started skating because he thought I must've been cheating on him. My sarcastic reply was, "Like, bruh, I was going skating regularly before us and I will continue to go skating after us, if this relationship doesn't last."

Funny story time. Before I bought my first pair of $500+ expensive skates, I used to straight kill it in rentals! There's a JB skate track produced by Chicago's owned DJ T-Rell that goes like, "... I'm in my zone, I'm killin' it!" Shout out to all the cold brownie skaters. I remember one night like it was yesterday. I was rolling at the rink, on the outside near the wall with the fast skaters, when this man came out of nowhere and said to me in a pimp-like voice, "Baby girl, it's about time you come up out of them." I was completely stunned. It was at that very moment I knew I had graduated onto the 'Who's Who Skaters Roster' and the session's regular skaters started watching.

Why do I skate? Let me be clear. I don't skate for the approval of others. People find pleasure and entertainment in witnessing my being in my drama-free zone. Now granted, I am a professional performing artist with a very strong dance background and resume, so I'm used to performing in front of an audience. I've been told on several occasions that I do some abnormal things that get people's attention when I'm not purposely trying to. For the most part, I don't mind the attention as long as it isn't from some creep. I skate simply because it makes my heart smile.

I fell even more in love with skating because of the music. OMG! I grew up listening to the original JB's (James Brown) tracks like "The Big Payback", "Hot Pants", "The Boss", "Gimme Some More", "Same Beat" and another classic such as "My Part/Make it Funky (parts 3 and 4), which was remixed by a Chicago producer known as Keezo Kane and he called it "Ga Ga Ga." Shout to all the JB skate DJs and producers who gave me life on my sk8s!

I consider myself a part of the 'middle-aged' skate generation. Growing up, I admired tagging behind a lot of skate legends in Chicago's rinks. Yet, I can hang with today's newer young skaters. I call them the 'Tasmanian devil' generation because of how daringly risky they skate without fear. Hands down, I love and respect them all. I think they are so freaking amazing and naturally talented. I adore watching them and love the adrenaline rush I get when rolling with all skate styles and generations. Honestly, to describe my skate style; it would have to be a combination of many styles, and not just JB because I'm from Chicago. I've absorbed styles I've seen and tried from many attending international skate parties and remember I definitely would throw in a lot of learned dance techniques.

Roller skating has opened up doors and given me many opportunities. I've been able to slay in my skates and perform for events like music videos, plays, birthday parties, parades, international skate jams, and be a part of various skate promotional material. One of my latest skate endeavors is being able to DJ for my skate community. I recall the first time I had the opportunity to co-DJ during an adult skate session and it was like falling in love again. I was nervous and excited at the same time, but it felt so good to see fellow skaters enjoy my mixes. I have always loved music and can listen to it for hours. I like all sorts of music genres, especially house, juke, and skate tracks. For me, it's the bass. I have had experience in the past, assisting with composing performance tracks for me, recording artists, and other dancers. As a DJ, I have spun for events like birthday parties, school assemblies, community events, mitzvahs, weddings, quinceaneras, radio shows, zoom parties, and silent headphone parties, to name a few.

Anything is possible when you follow your passion(s) while putting your God-given talent to good use. My advice to anyone who receives it, not just skaters, is to do you no matter what's going on around you.

Do You Know...

## Roller Skating Records

Roller skating enthusiasts are continually pushing the boundaries and setting new records in various categories. One of the most notable records in the world of roller skating is the longest distance traveled on roller skates in a twenty-four-hour period. Skaters attempt to cover as much ground as possible within a single day, testing their endurance and stamina. These endurance challenges often take place on tracks or courses specifically designed for long-distance skating, with participants skating continuously for hours on end.

Roller skating enthusiasts also strive to achieve records in speed skating, competing to set the fastest times over specific distances, such as 100 meters or one mile, on both traditional quad skates and inline skates. Speed skating events attract skilled athletes who train rigorously to maximize their speed and agility on the track, often reaching impressive velocities that rival those of other fast-paced sports.

Some roller skating records are more unconventional and showcase the creativity and ingenuity of participants. For example, skaters may attempt to set records for the most consecutive hours spent roller skating or the most complex and intricate roller skating routines performed in a single session. These records often require a combination of skill, determination, and teamwork, as participants work together to achieve their goals while pushing the boundaries of what is possible on roller skates.

Roller skating records captivate audiences around the world, inspiring admiration and awe for the incredible feats accomplished by skaters of all ages and backgrounds. Whether it's breaking a long-standing distance record, setting a new speed record, or achieving a unique and unconventional feat, roller skating enthusiasts continue to push themselves to new heights in pursuit of their passion for the sport. These records serve as a testament to the dedication, talent, and spirit of the roller skating community, showcasing the boundless potential of human achievement on wheels.

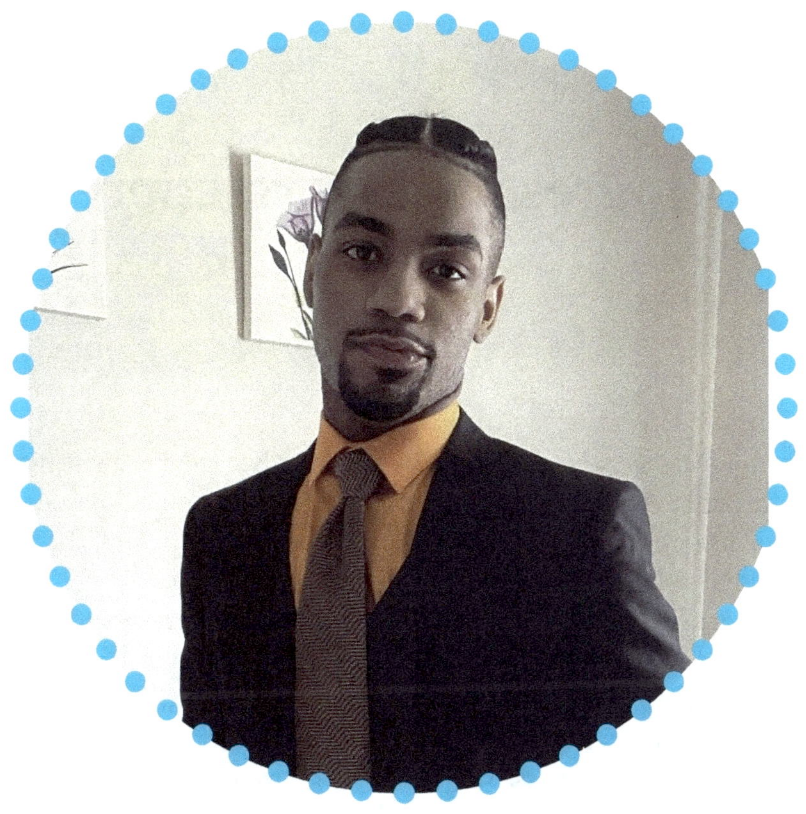

*Nicholas N. Moore*

Facebook: @Nick Moore | Instagram: @nick_so_slick89

# "Progress Not Perfection"

*Progression, not perfection,* is the mantra that has acted as a touchstone throughout my life. I was born in 1989 in St. Louis, Missouri. In 1989, Chicago's skating rinks like The Loop, Rainbow, and The Rink were hubs for Black Chicago skaters of that generation. In 1989, at two weeks old, my family migrated to Chicago to live with my grandparents, who would become my foundation. Twenty years later, I started my skate journey in 2009 when I accompanied a friend to The Rink on a Chicago December Sunday night. It was what Chicagoans call a JB set. People dressed to impress. The music was powerful, and I fell in love instantly. I did not have a car and my housing situation was not stable. I depended on a friend for movement around the city, so I did my best to keep my friend engaged in skating because I knew I wanted to be a part of this community. I started researching skate sessions around the city. I purchased my first pair of skates: Chicago Skates and the first "move" I learned was the eagle spread. This was the beginning of what is now an eleven-year adoration for the culture and the community. Both my friend and I continue to skate. My friend started his own skate group and I enjoy skating individually and with friends.

Skating has impacted my life in many ways. Although I am not a competitive skater and rarely participate in official skate competitions, I have won some local events. At Rich City Skate, Inc, a skating rink that has since closed, I participated in a competition that was hosted by Chicago's Most Wanted (CMW) skate group. I was reluctant to enter with his uncle Poochie. Still a relatively new skater, I had not yet built

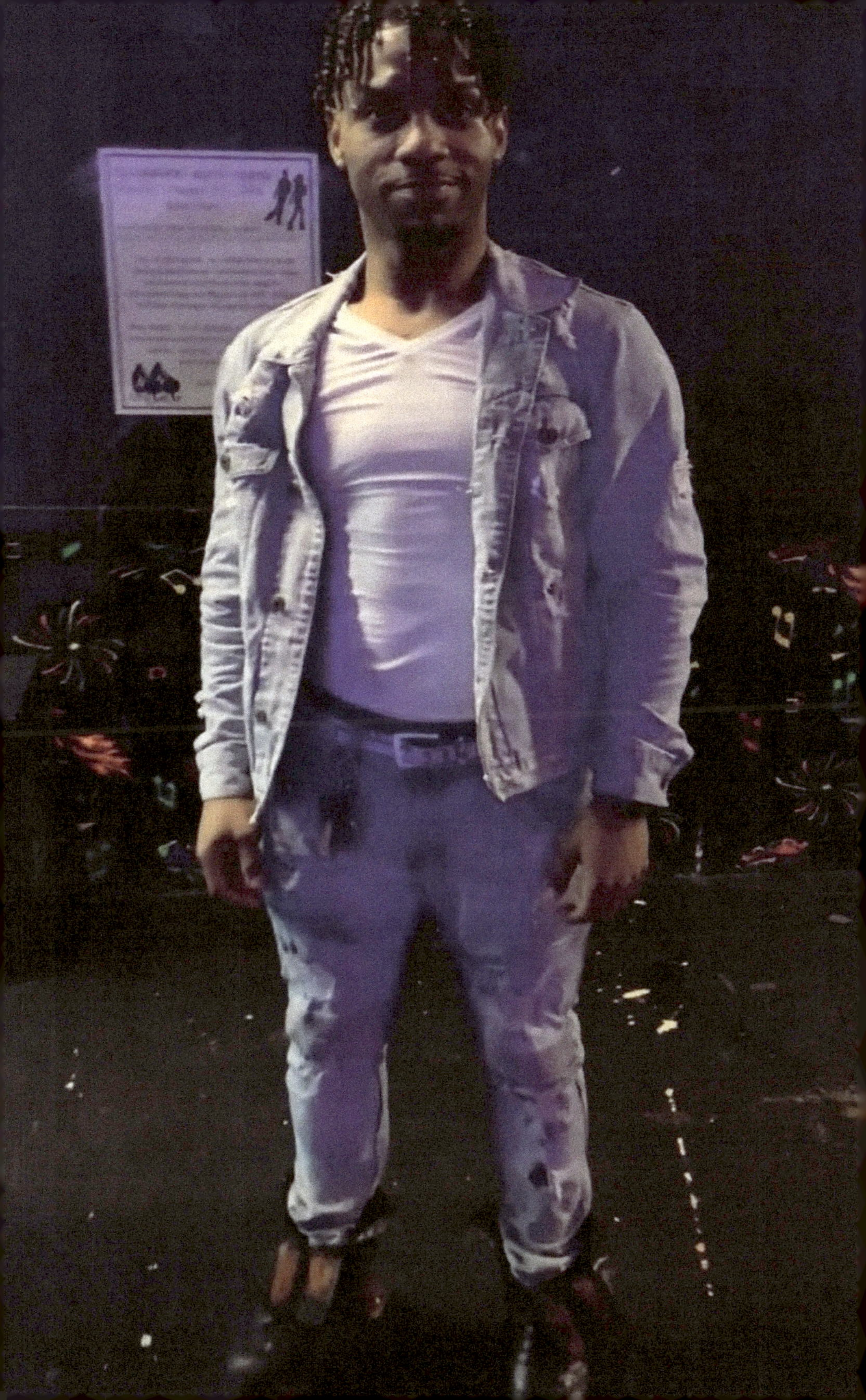

the confidence I felt I needed. Poochie motivated me to participate, and we ended up winning the competition. The thing that made our skate duo stand out against the other skaters was that we skated on "the edge" and in "the middle." Skating is more than an activity. It is a culture. Skate groups are an experience that is common to new skaters. I was a member of A&S skate group and learned and met a variety of people in the community. Skating provides many with the opportunity to expand their social and professional networks as well as travel to large skate events domestically and abroad. As an individual, skating has been a constant. My skates have been with me through adversity and advancement. Skating is filled with "skate parties." These can range from local to international, but they always draw large crowds, video footage that is shared, and reputations are either made or maintained. In Chicago, there is an annual Halloween skate party at The Rink. This event draws a large crowd each year. During this particular event, people skate around "the edge" and in "the middle." Learning both styles, I debuted my "middle work" this night. Needless to say, I killed it! This has been one of my most memorable experiences. I was able to overcome my fear of being the center of attention. It acted as a boost of confidence. Sometimes trauma can lead a person to retreat into self. Skating can be an individual activity while simultaneously being a community activity. It can also be a place and space where people feel as if their insecurities are front and center. Depending on how a person processes the skate time and space, these pressures can motivate or alienate. In this instance, it motivated. After this experience, I felt more confident and acknowledged by other skaters and those I looked up to. I felt empowered to come out of my comfort zone and push the boundaries. Skate traveling increased, and I was becoming more familiar with the skate culture outside of Chicago and beyond JB. This was a turning point.

For many Black males, especially in Chicago, trauma is something they either do not address or address it through damaging means. Skaters vent through their footwork and artistry. Although skating has an addictive quality, the more a person goes the more he or she wants to go back, it is not damaging. Coming out of college, I was not certain about my life's direction. I wanted some excitement and needed stability. I've experienced homelessness and grief, but skating has been an outlet. My grandmother transitioned when I was eighteen years old, and someone murdered my father when I was sixteen years old. Learning to cope and survive early, skating was a means to stay on a positive path, stay away from drugs and crime, and focus on something other than coping and surviving. A typical skate session is four hours long. Sometimes I would have $10.00 and chose to skate because I knew that for those four hours, I could escape the realities of my grief and my unstable living situation. The skate community would not let me go hungry. Skating and skaters fed me physically and emotionally. Someone always had an extra $5.00 or was "going my way" to give me a ride home if needed. The impact skating has had and continues to have on my life exceeds words.

# Do You Know...

## Roller Skating and Fashion

Roller skating fashion has always been a reflection of the vibrant and dynamic culture surrounding the sport. During the disco era of the 1970s, skaters embraced flamboyant attire, featuring sequins, glitter, and metallic fabrics that shimmered under the disco lights. Neon colors, spandex leggings, and oversized accessories defined the roller skating fashion of the 1980s, mirroring the bold and exuberant spirit of the decade.

In the 1990s, roller skating fashion took on a grunge-inspired look, with skaters favoring casual and laid-back attire such as baggy jeans, flannel shirts, and oversized T-shirts. Roller skating rinks became gathering places where skaters could express themselves through their fashion choices, embracing the influence of alternative rock and hip-hop music on youth culture.

Today, roller skating fashion continues to evolve, with skaters drawing inspiration from a diverse range of sources, including streetwear, vintage fashion, and athletic apparel. Customization and personalization play a significant role, allowing skaters to express their individuality and creativity through their attire and accessories. Whether channeling the glamour of past decades or embracing contemporary trends, roller skating fashion remains a vibrant and integral part of the roller skating experience, celebrating the spirit of self-expression and creativity on wheels.

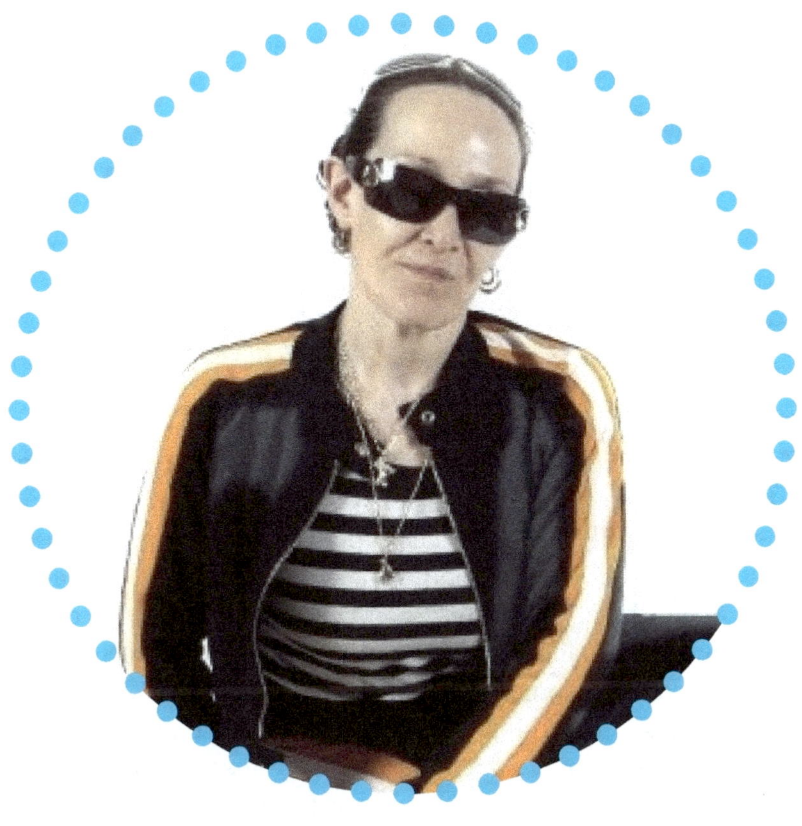

Joanna Andrew

Facebook: @Joanna Andrew

# "Hot Steppin' Granny"

You cannot imagine the incredible journey you are about to embark upon when you put on your first pair of roller skates. The people you will meet, the places you will go, and the changes that will happen to you in mind, body, and spirit. You will find reserves of determination and dedication coming from within you that you never knew existed and you will feel passion, love, and joy as you continue to skate. Eventually, you will blossom and glow, as the light that has always been within you begins to shine. Every minute you spend skating is a minute spent caring for yourself, which can only be a good thing. So much can come from one choice: to slip your feet eagerly into a waiting pair of roller skates. But beware, the dark side—vanity, over-competitiveness, and ego—can be all-consuming if you do not keep it in check. What you put out into the Universe will return. Thoughts become actions, which become a state of being. Man is measured by his deeds, not by his words. So, tend to your light side—always. Be good—do good. Yin cannot exist without Yang and thus, you will become a whole and well-balanced person if you follow this way of being.

Your journey will naturally be different from mine. All I can recount are my own experiences. I'm known on the Internet and in skating circuits as Hot Stepping Granny. You can find my YouTube here: http://uk.youtube.com/HotSteppingGranny. My channel has a wealth of free resources for those wishing to learn or improve their skating. It also showcases many of our English skaters, so you can get to know them. In person, I offer roller skating premises analysis and a

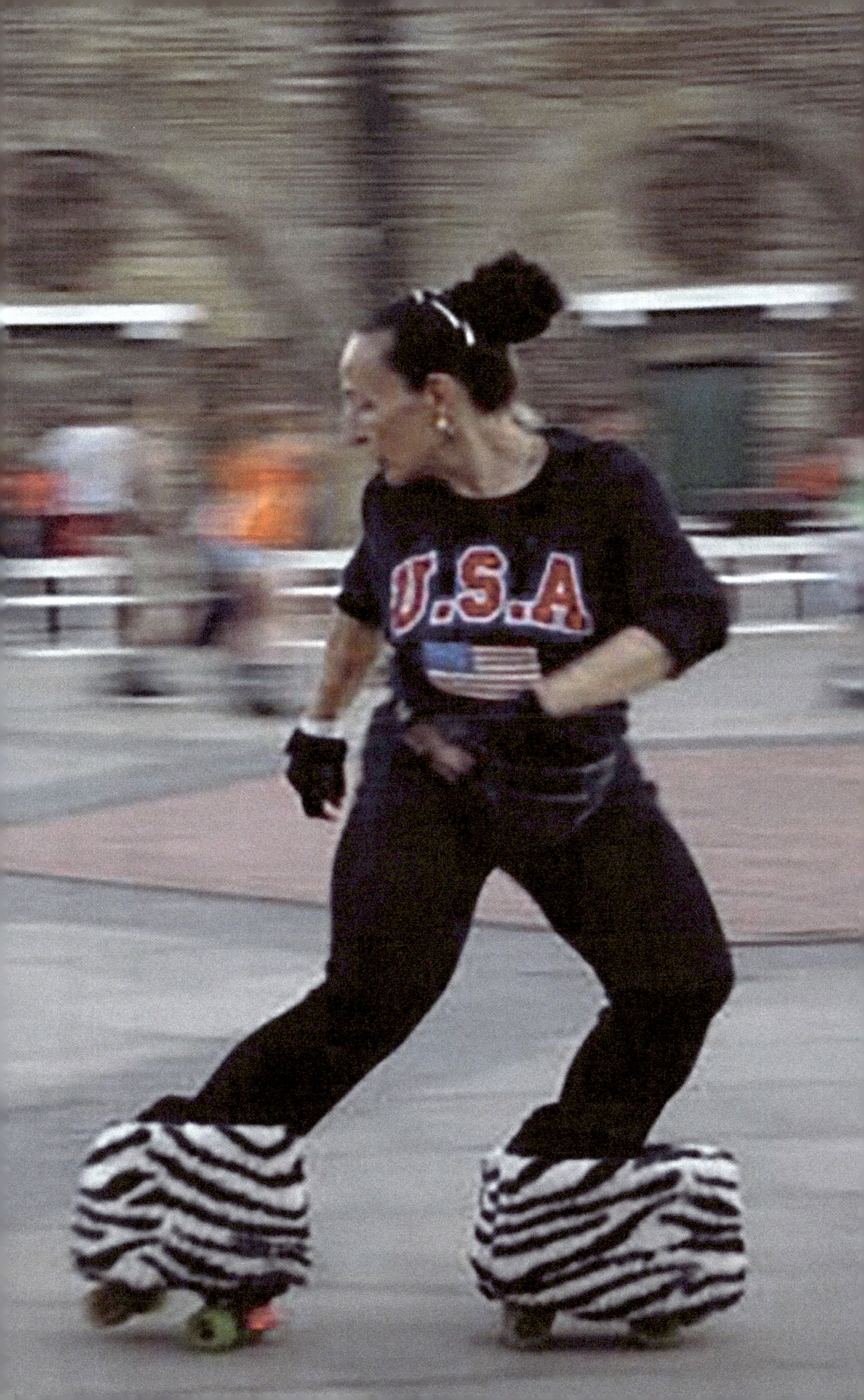
U.S.A

risk assessment consultancy service to those wishing to open skating premises, in accordance with our Local Government Health & Safety Laws, which encompass health and safety and best practice training for client care and floor staff. I do this for free. This ensures that our rinks and skating clubs are safe spaces for people to skate in and work at and ultimately, so that the sport/art/state of being that I love so dearly can live on for future generations of roller-skaters.

Over the years, I have contributed a great deal to my community, from blogging, forum running, providing free resources, writing and roving reportage for skating magazines, finding work for skaters, training floor staff, volunteering, skate instructing and ultimately writing formal Health & Safety Reports and Staff Training documentation for local councils, which enabled Roller Disco, Canvas, and the Renaissance Rooms, Vauxhall to safely open and run as long-standing and successful skating venues, which laid the foundation for Roller Nation, Bruce Grove to open as an ongoing concern. I have taught more people to skate than I can remember, in person and via video, and inspired (I hope) a great many more. For if I can do it, anyone can. It is my intention for my contribution to help standardize roller floor staff best practices (marshals/skate guards/instructors) and for employees to provide a safe place to work and for their clients to skate. If skating venues are properly run, their doors will be open for many years to come.

We have many skating stars who shine like precious jewels. My opinion is that stars need a nurturing place from which to shine and to be truly appreciated. I'm a nineties rink-skating, swing-back skating, freestyle dancer. You can tell UK rink skaters by the foam boot cushions we wear around our skates, which protect them and us from falls, knocks, dings, drops, and scrapes. I have many pairs of vintage hockey skates, which are still worn and protected in this way. I do have speed and figure boots, but I'm happier on hockey skates.

I have always loved to roller skate. I fell in love with roller skating at four years old, skating on the sidewalk outside my home. By ten, I was old enough to skate at our local roller rink. I also joined an artistic skating club at eleven. At eighteen, I discovered roller dancing at a local nightclub. In my early thirties, a new rink opened. I thought I'd died and gone to heaven. I skated there every week until it closed in the summer of 1997. Roller Disco, Canvas opened in 2004. I eventually became their head skate guard and health and safety officer, having responsibility for both venues—Roller Disco, Canvas, and the Renaissance Rooms, Vauxhall. I left in 2009. The owner sought me out to assist at a new venue he was opening: Rollernation at Bruce Grove. I became the skate instructor for their family sessions in 2020 and left in 2022. I can only describe roller skating as something akin to a spark in my soul; always silently smoldering. Sometimes it urges me to let it burn and let loose with passion and ferocity. Sometimes it urges me to bathe in the light of the more cooling aspect of its flame. It can be an all-consuming passion and terribly addictive. As with everything, balance is key. Tend to the training of your body and your mind.

Roller skating has impacted my life considerably. I would not be the woman that I am today without it. I have changed and grown and matured immeasurably because I roller skate. If one considers skating to be a pie—everybody wants a piece of it. If everybody is busy chowing down on that pie, pretty soon the pie tin becomes empty. I am a pie maker. Our community needs more pie makers! I was the most unlikely one of my age group among my peers to become a roller skater; much less one worthy of note. I was short, round, and bespectacled. I never quite fit in and I'm not particularly photogenic anyhow. I have suffered for my art and that's okay because skating has made me strong, resilient, and an incredibly deep thinker. You cannot see this just by looking at me and that's okay, too. I have had an interesting life journey fraught with sadness and woes—three failed marriages, two nervous breakdowns, and I have raised a biological daughter, a stepson, and two of my four grandchildren (both boys). Skating has always been there for my family and me to share and enjoy, and we have all had many happy days skating and having fun in the most unlikely of places. Skating has ensured that all my young charges grew up fit, strong, confident, and as balanced as they could be in terms of being individuals and it has helped to prepare them for whatever life may bring their way.

There have also been many good points in my journey. I have been blessed with some truly wonderful opportunities, good friends, and a wonderful fiancé whom I love dearly. Being a dedicated roller skater has given me strength and discipline. I have changed physically, losing seventy-seven pounds. It has brought balance to my life when it has been exceptionally chaotic. It has given me clarity of thought and added another way of seeing the world. I have matured and become a much better and more spiritual person because of my skating. I take prescription medication for depression and anxiety. I also meditate daily. I have been clean and sober now for well over thirty years, not that I ever had a problem with that sort of stuff anyway.

Skating represents an altered state of being. For me, it is art and sport and incredibly spiritual. I do not like to skate without music. Music is key. When I'm on skates, I become one in mind, body, and spirit; all that matters is the music and movement in that moment and I am at peace from whatever is going on in my mind or the world. When you are on skates you move differently, take chances, and think faster and more clearly as you have a small space surrounding you in which to move, to radiate your energy, to project, and to be. Your skating self is very different from your static self. You flow. Consequently, your inner self radiates and you can interpret what you hear (the music) with your body (via means of dance and movement). You bare your soul and your inner light becomes visible. Those who share your passion have eyes to see it. At that moment, the light within you recognizes the light within me and we are one—the true meaning of "NAMASTE." It does not matter your station in life, race, creed, age, religion, or color for skating is a great leveler, which transcends all barriers. Those who do not have eyes to see this, don't and that's okay.

The 2020 lockdown was awful here, but it did English roller skaters a huge favor. When the lockdown was lifted, more people than I had ever seen had taught themselves to roller dance, as they had the time on their hands to dedicate themselves to learning to do so.

A skating rink is so much more than a place to skate. It's part place of worship, part gym, a place to meet new friends and old, a place of community, a spiritual place, a place of energy, a place to dance, a place to safely let loose, a place to practice, a place of belonging, and a place of mutual respect. A skating rink ultimately takes on a life of its own. It becomes a shared collective, where everyone can experience the same vibe, in their own unique way, while exchanging inflowing and outflowing energies, which leaves the body glowing and the soul refreshed.

I can only use the analogy of those old Shaw Brothers Kung Fu movies. There are great debates over which style is the best. Some masters follow the way of the Iron Fist, some the Drunken Gods, some the Mantis, some the Snake, and some the Tiger. Each genre has much to prove and challenges and often battles ensue. Oh, my stars, the arguments I've had with people online and in person over this point. And I've had some incredible dance battles in my time. This is because my generation had some very vocal inline skaters seeking to attempt to reinvent the wheel! I represent quad skating and roller dance with a passion—very hard and very loud. It didn't exactly make me many friends, and that's okay as I stood up for what I believed in, with the passion and ferocity of a British Bulldog. I am of age now (sixty-two at the time of writing) where the only battle I have is with myself. I strive to become better than I was yesterday, as a person and a skater. This is because with age, comes wisdom. The core from which all styles come is one's Chi (the flow of internal energy). The more we skate, the more we become fitter and our bodies can respond to external stimuli with incredible balance and accuracy. No matter what sort of music one likes to skate to and no matter what genre of skating one prefers, we all have core energy (Chi) and we all become fit.

We are all skaters, no matter our preferences and there is room in the Universe for us all. Roller skating has evolved to where it is no longer a male-dominated sport here and it is wonderful to see lady skaters treated with respect, as skaters of skill in their own right. Things were not like that when I came up through the ranks and I never much cared for the limelight that came with skating well anyhow. I shall leave the joys of filming, photo shoots, and casting calls to our younger skaters to add to their portfolios. Please believe me when I say that our younger skaters are a true joy to behold and I have spent many happy hours delighting in watching them blossom and grow. The way they skate is incredible and I cannot wait to see what future generations of skaters bring to our community.

We are so lucky here in London, England, as we now have two places at which to skate regularly: Rollernation, in Bruce Grove, Tottenham, which is a roller skating nightclub, and Flipper's Roller

Boogie Palace, in Shepherd's Bush, Central London, which is a rink and a roller skating nightclub, with a restaurant and skate shop.

My fiancé's health is not the best at the moment. He is waiting for several surgeries, so I'm pretty much his legs until he can get around to doing things under his own steam. This has kept me pretty busy. I don't have as much time to dedicate to my skating as I would like. But I stretch, lift weights, cycle, walk and dance, so basic routine maintenance keeps my body flexible and working like it's supposed to. When I get out to skate, I generally roll at Flipper's. It's so welcoming and I love to dance about in my little spot, bar-side, practicing my footwork in the mirrors there. I enjoy watching others roll as much as I love to skate. Our younger skaters are so incredibly talented and it fills my heart with joy to see this new generation of skaters as in love with the sport as I am and ever was. Now and then, we might catch each other's eye and smile, that all-knowing "Namaste" smile, where light recognizes light, showing respect and appreciation for each other. I feel honored and blessed to have experienced these moments in life and am humbled and grateful to have been able to contribute to the future and the well-being of my community. I would not have been able to do so without first having slipped my feet into a welcoming pair of roller skates.

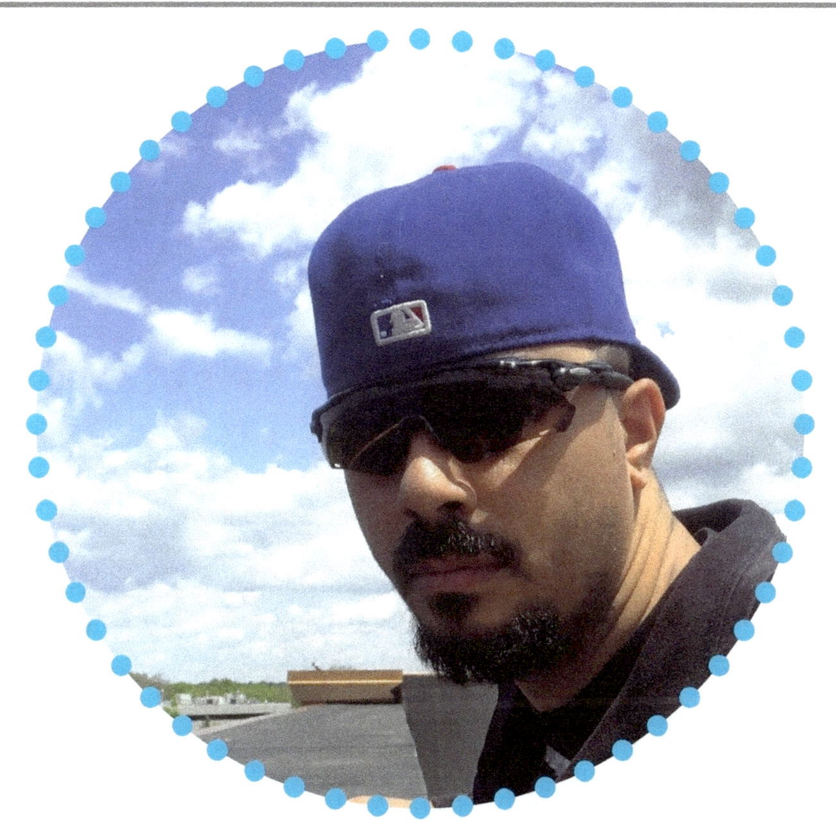

Christopher Paul Morales

Facebook: @Christopher Paul Morales

Instagram: @the_experience_paul_morales

# "Being Humble in the Skate World"

Let's get one thing clear. My story is to educate and open your mind to the world and the art of skating. Yes, skating.

Growing up in New York City, there was not a lot to do when I was younger. A time where riots and violence took place almost every day put a damper on what was possible. Skating was my only outlet. At two years old, I believe it was my destiny to achieve greatness as a skater, but learning an art form is not as easy as one may think. It takes hard work, dedication, time, and learning from great people/coaches who have perfected the craft.

I started as an ice skater at Kate Wollman Rink in Prospect Park in Brooklyn, two blocks from the Empire Rollerdrome. I wanted to understand the art of edge work. Learning different forms and understanding how edge work is very important to a skater. It's the fundamentals. I favored ice dancing because of the deep edge work of some dances. It's focused on posture or form, proper weight distribution, and Wollman—the understanding of how to use your edge to complete the movement. Now skating is universal and edge work is edge work. Period!

It's the stroke, not the stride. Ice/figure skaters stroke down the ice by using their weight and posture and applying it to their edges. So, I made it my goal to master those dances/movements. I could still complete different movements such as movements in the field. I also became an excellent hockey player! Playing for different organizations in New York City, I took what I learned as a figure skater and applied it to the game of hockey. Hockey players learn edge work from figure skaters. Overall, it expanded my view and understanding of edge work.

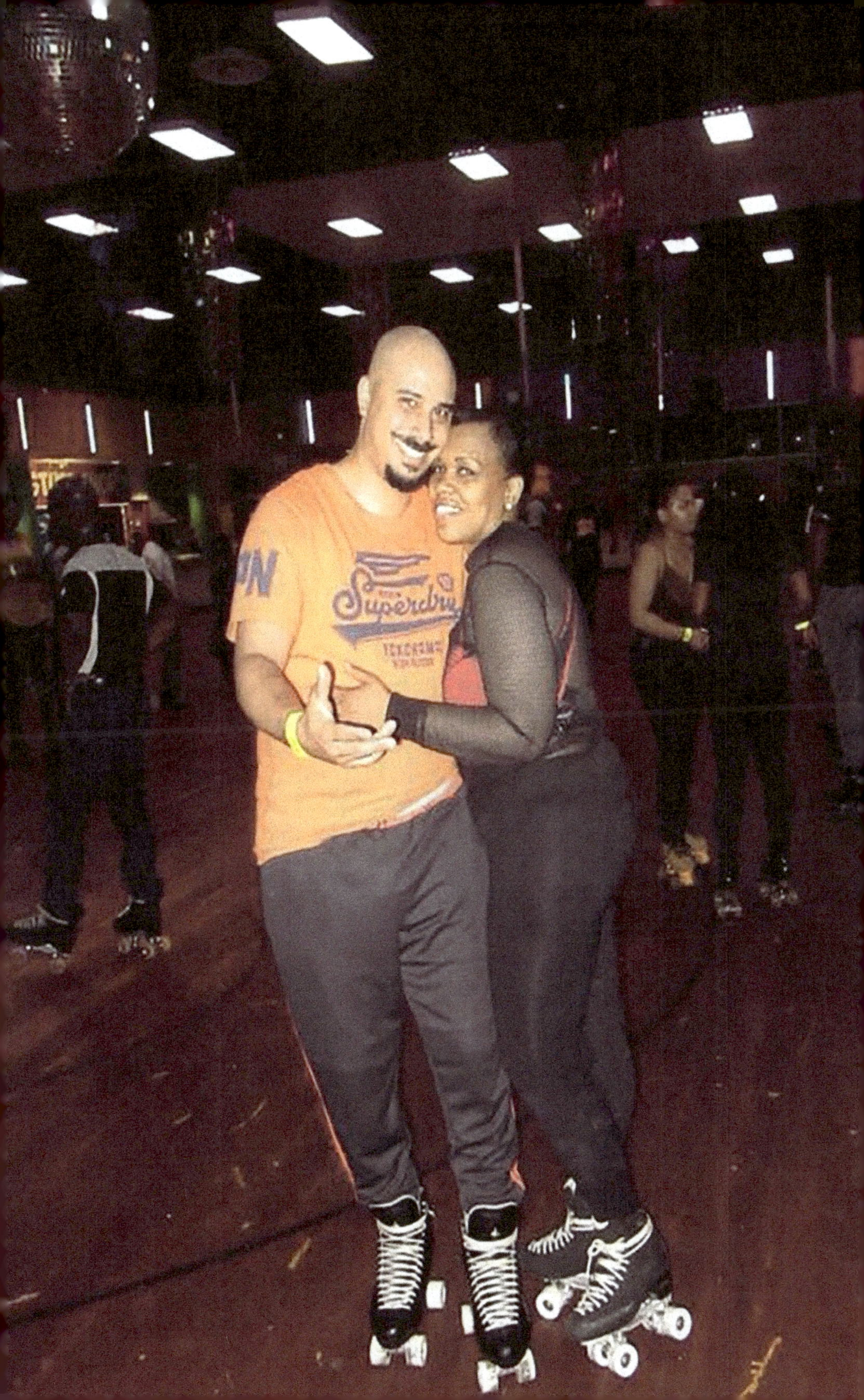
Superdry

Now the transformation of a roller skater! How can I transform what I have learned into my own style? I did not understand what a stride was. Skate to the beat. Placement. Pivot left and right side. Under and over, etc. No idea. I started with rollerblades. Yes, at Empire Rollerdrome and the Skate Key in New York City. I also worked as a floor guard. A great friend and brother, Eric Alston, said, "Put these on and I bet you won't skate on anything else." After that one night, I was hooked. Besides the music, it blew my mind. After that, my roller skate journey began. It was very hard.

I earned the right to skate with the adult crowd. Back in the day, you had to earn it. I was so driven by what I saw and experienced; I made it my goal. I skated five to six nights a week. I didn't stop; I was too hungry. So, I sought to be educated by the best. Even traveling to New Jersey to Skate 22 and the rink in Bergenfield.

I met Bill Butler, the godfather of roller disco, and the creator of the Jammin technique. I saw something I never saw before. Style! The Jammin technique in its raw form. I couldn't believe it. The edgework was crazy. I had no words, but I knew it was what I wanted to learn and master. Bill Butler, Mike Johnson, Sandy, Eric Alston, Noriko, Lenny, Antonio, Randy, Solomon, Kurby Brown, James, Mr. Charles, Amy Ellis, Will, Jimmy, and Ice from Philadelphia were my mentors. I invested in time, equipment, and technique. I stopped for no one. I was like a sponge and that's all I wanted to do! They pushed me harder than most and I felt I needed to be pushed to greatness in my own way! Not for recognition from others, but to say I achieved at an art form that was truly inspirational and showed my full potential!

Everyone kept saying, "Keep your head up." That was my biggest problem. I started with the basic understanding of a pivot and the understanding of the plow and how to incorporate that movement into the Jammin technique. It was hard. Bend your knees. Shifting your weight. Placement. I would not give up. I had the best mentors and the best tools at my disposal. Stride after stride, plow after plow, hockey stops after hockey stops, learning how to control my weight when skating with a partner, the exchange of power and understanding skating in the pocket, and learning how to skate on both sides. That was hard. It was a challenge. Staying hungry got me to the level I'm at today.

I started traveling a lot to skating events. Atlanta, North Carolina, Philadelphia, and other states and saw other skate styles. A lot of people don't know that I was the first to bring the JB Style and fast backward to New York City. I put Boston on the map at Chez Vous. I started adult and ladies' night as a DJ. Going from rink to rink opened my eyes even more. The styles were unique and the music behind the styles was shocking. The remixes and skate movements opened the gates for creativity.

I traveled with Big Bob and Eric Alston. Helping from time to time with record carrying and even cleaning the rink floor! I cared about how clean the floors were at Empire and Skate Key. Before every adult night at Empire, I mopped and swept the rink floor and the same at Skate Key. Understanding how an event of a session should be, the understanding of how lighting effectively changed the mood for skaters, and the overall experience were mind-blowing!

I fell on some hard times and thought my energy and passion were going to be affected. I knew people didn't want me to succeed because the drama started. To be very honest, it made me a much stronger person and a skater. I was a part of skate groups and relationships that eventually fell apart and I was okay with that. I said to myself, "How can I be great by myself?" So, I continued to practice more than ever and didn't care what people thought about me. I traveled and traveled and gained more and more experience. If it weren't for Eric Alston and Mike Johnson, I don't know where I would be today! They took me under their wings and groomed me more than anyone! Mike used to have small skate sessions, which was a serious workout. If you think what you do now is something, skate with Mike during a skate session. Eric's workout was mental and physical on and off the skate floor. They both taught me the value of ethics and respect for other skaters and styles. Both were great mentors and never gave up on me! I remember always talking with Ice at barbecues and right before we hit the floor. We had a blast doing open house and splits in the corners, during sessions, which was the norm for us.

I started teaching here and there. I realized that the skate world is bigger than all of us. Stay humble and keep your head up! Keep an open mind.

You don't know it all. Skate for those that can't and understand the art for what it is in its raw form. The overall technique will blow your mind if you can get over your ego. You're not great for doing a bunch of moves or tricks if that's what you want to call it. It's how you pass on the knowledge that makes you great. People say that I'm a living legend in the skate world. I say I had my time and I will continue to skate for those that have fallen and for those that can't! Take what you have learned and embrace it like a newborn baby!

As a DJ, I have strived to be different with selections of records and how I play them. Watching Big Bob, Ekim, Antonio, and some other great DJs from The Loft and the Paradise Garage days because of my mother's dancing career in those clubs and studios. I believe every record tells a story like skating. With every stride and movement, it's says something about you! I remember when one DJ held down the whole night and now it's four or more! It's to each his own! I'm very old school when it comes to deejaying. Smooth blends and playing records you don't or haven't heard anymore. Listening to great DJs from the past has embraced me and help me understand the art of deejaying and how skating is alike. Always digging into the past and bring it to the present. Just like skating. Now for the new jacks, don't think what you're doing is something new! The movements and techniques were around way before you ever started. All you're doing is putting your twist to it. That doesn't mean you invented it. You just changed the game for yourself and that is your version of self-expression in the art of roller skating. Truth. Can't handle it? Sorry!

Besides, being thrown from one side of the rink to the other taught me the value of control. Empire and the Key took me in like it was meant to be! I stayed positive and focus. I felt like I was a part of a second family. I met a lot of great skaters along the way! A lot of them I stay in contact with to this day! Trust and believe, if you could skate at the Key in the Bronx, you can skate anywhere.

At the end of the day, start humble and stay true to yourself. Don't let anything stop you from your goals. Learn to listen to others that have paved the way for you! If you're not able to let go of your ego and pride, then you will never achieve the level of mastery that some have. I believe I have but all good masters of any art form continue to learn!

I have been very lucky to turn a passion into a career. I have been in the ice rink industry for over twenty years. I'm considered a rink operator or an ice technician. I have helped build skating programs for the boys and girls clubs in Bronx, New York, and other organizations. I have also helped build and design a few ice rinks permanent and semi-permanent (indoor and outdoor). Finally, I met my best friend and beautiful wife, Towanda Morales!

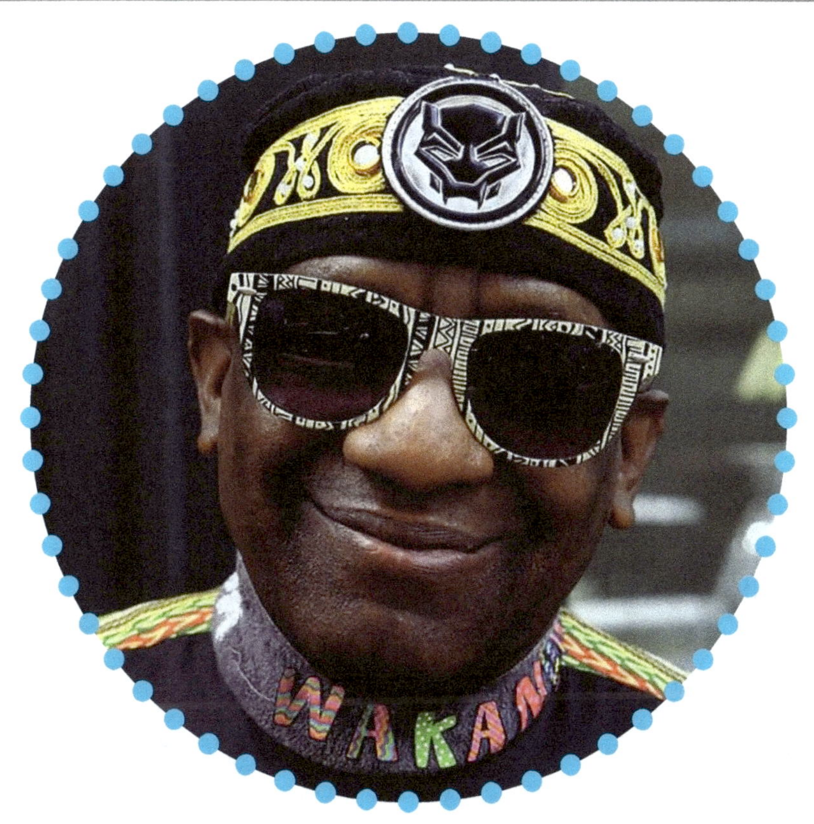

## Harry R. Gaskin

Facebook: @Harry R Gaskin | Instagram: @Harry.r.gaskin

# "Energy in the Middle"

I'm head of the dance roller skating team called Energy in the Middle. I believe in positive thinking. I believe in turning lemons into lemonade. My mottos are: "Never give up". "If you don't use it, you will lose it." "Don't let anyone stop you from achieving your goal." My goal is to promote the art of dance roller skating. I base my style of dance roller skating on Michael Jackson, Soul Train, The Nicholas Brothers, James Brown, and the Lockers.

I went from the tenement to the housing projects to a house to a great apartment building. Life is a roller coaster. There are always ups and downs. I started skating at the age of ten in the housing projects. I served in the United States Army. I have a B.A. and an M.A. in art education. I was a museum educator for the Studio Museum in Harlem. I was an art teacher for the New York Board of Education. I'm a Vietnam-era veteran and a freelance cartoonist. I took Taekwondo while in the Army.

When I came out of military service, tragedy hit my close-knit family hard. My sister and nephew were stabbed to death by her husband. We had to break into their apartment with the super. My father, mother, and I saw the result close up. We later learned he had taken marijuana with angel dust.

Only my belief in God kept me going strong. It was news coverage for the wrong reasons.

One day in the late1970s, I was walking in Central Park. I saw the roller skaters dancing on their skates. Wayne and Starr would set

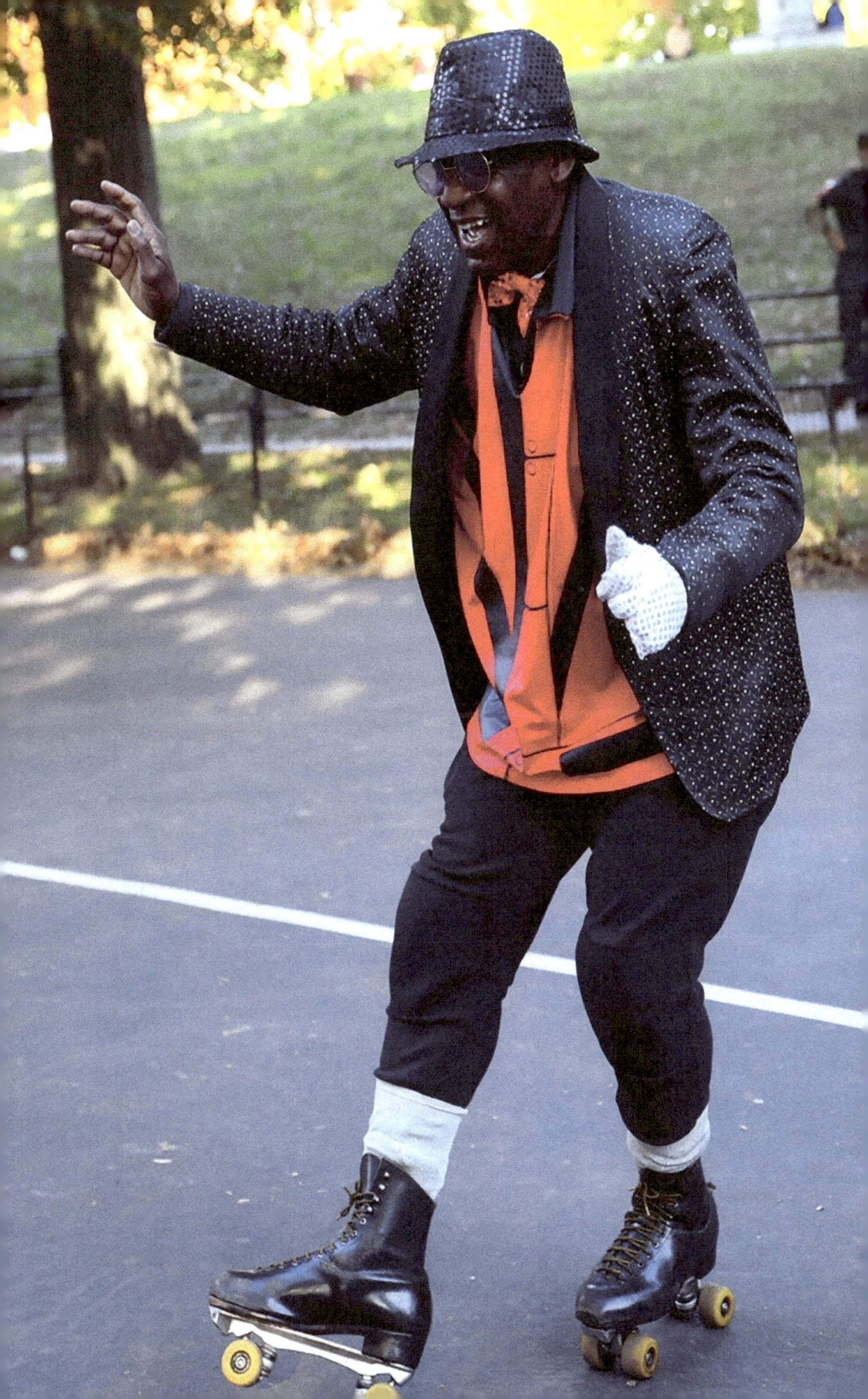

up their boom boxes in the middle of 72nd. We would dance-skate to their music. I fell in love with roller skating. I used to play basketball, football, baseball, martial arts, tennis. Nothing has given me more joy than roller skating. Soon I was going to the different indoor roller rinks. Empire, Skate Key, Laces, the Rink, Wollman Rink, Roxy, Hotskates, Manhattan Skates, Skate 22, United Skates, High Rollers, the Rooftop, and Central Park Skate Circle.

One day, in one of the roller skating rinks, I started making up steps and routines. I turned around and to my surprise, there were twenty skaters following me. I was shocked and happy. I soon started creating line dances on roller skates. Soon, many skaters were doing my skate routines with me.

The next thing I knew, in 2010, I won the Adrenalin Award Best Dance Roller Skater Choreographer in the country.

My skate team is called Energy in the Middle. We are about health and fitness. We are a dynamic group of dance roller skaters. We are full of excitement and lively enthusiasm. The essence of fitness and fun. We travel to skate, perform, and compete at various venues across the country. We have performed or competed at schools, museums, senior centers, parks, music videos, on television, parades, and in movies, including "Gotta Get Myself Into It" by Rapture music video, 2010 winner of the McDonald's Gospel Fest in praise dance on roller skate, New York State Championship in "Roll Bounce" dance roller skate competition, performed in the African American day parades, the Apollo theater Harlem summer stage, Peace and WHCR and WBLS radio performances, 98.7 Kiss FM cares coat Drives, gospel celebrations, Disney Street games performance, YMCA Skates shows for fitness, "Saturday " by De LA Soul music video, Village Halloween parades, Central Park Dance Skate Association skate shows, New York safe night out by NYPD, Roll Bounce movie red carpet and special feature performance, Barkley Kalpak tour company, Metro Health Fair, Minisink Townhouse, show for homeless children, The Museum of the City of New York, 98 Mott, HBO Mixtapes, and Roller skates - Movies: Pelham 123, American Gangster, Meteor, Just the Ticket, and Family Fang. ~Promotion Performances for America's Got Talent, Big Apple Minute on Fox 5, Good Day New York, Studio Museum in Harlem, and the Long Island Cares for Veterans TV special.

I would like to thank my Energy in the Middle teammates. I couldn't have done it without them: Denise Thomas, Terry Davis, Edna Davoll, Charlene Gary, Terri Murray, Horace Davis, Chera'e Ward, Michelle Davis, Adrienne West, Gwen White, Carl Bacote, Sweet and Low, Frankie Gaston, Paula Tinseley, Amy Ellis, Ronnie Johnson, Mary Mitchell, Gregory Freeman, Tia, Baron, Frank, Ronda, Joy, Lisa, and Bill White.

I also want to thank all the other amazing roller skaters who have done my skate routines with me over the years. You have given me so much joy. I love the look on skaters' faces when they finally get the routines right.

I enjoyed teaching roller skating. I have taught roller skating for the New York Board of Education. I have taught skating to middle school and high school. I'm proud to be part of Energy in the Middle dance roller skating team. I'm proud to be part of the Central Park Dance Skate Association. CPDSA has performed and served the community and tourism trade for years. I've also won many Halloween costumes contests using my skill as an artist and the ability to create.

# Do You Know...

## Roller Skating Museums

Roller skating enthusiasts have a haven in dedicated museums that celebrate the sport's rich history and culture. One prominent example is the National Roller Skating Museum in Lincoln, Nebraska, which stands as a testament to the enduring legacy of roller skating. Within its walls, visitors can explore a treasure trove of artifacts, memorabilia, and exhibits that offer a captivating journey through the evolution of roller skating over the years.

The National Roller Skating Museum serves as a comprehensive archive, preserving and showcasing significant moments and milestones in roller skating history. From vintage roller skates and equipment to photographs, posters, and documents, the museum's collection provides invaluable insights into the sport's origins and development. Visitors can immerse themselves in the nostalgia of bygone eras while gaining a deeper appreciation for roller skating's cultural significance.

Through its exhibits and displays, the museum pays tribute to the pioneers, innovators, and trailblazers who have shaped the world of roller skating. Visitors can learn about key figures in roller skating history, including inventors, athletes, and advocates who have left an indelible mark on the sport. From the earliest roller skate patents to iconic moments in roller derby and artistic skating, the museum offers a comprehensive overview of roller skating's evolution and impact.

In addition to preserving the past, the National Roller Skating Museum also celebrates the present and future of roller skating. Special exhibitions highlight contemporary trends, achievements, and advancements in the sport, ensuring that roller skating remains a vibrant and evolving cultural phenomenon. Whether you're a seasoned skater or a curious newcomer, a visit to the museum offers a fascinating glimpse into the rich heritage and enduring appeal of roller skating.

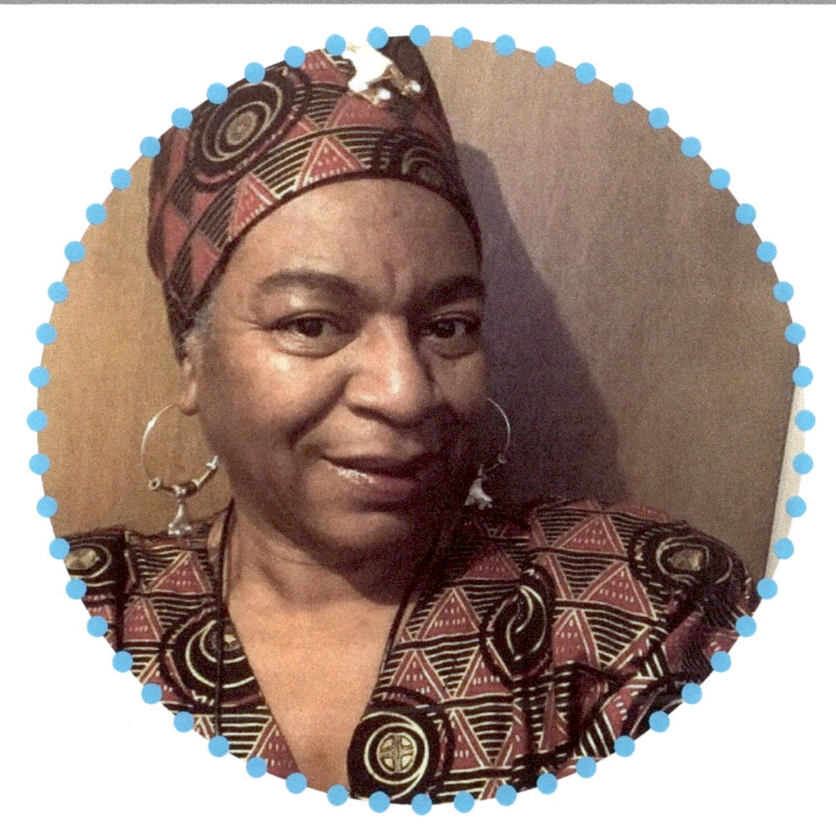

Marilyn Coleman

aka Socks

Facebook: @Marilyn Socks Coleman | Instagram: @socksrollin

# "Rollin' Through Six Decades with Socks from the 'D'"

What an honor it is to be amongst such an awesome Skate Family of Legends!

My nickname "Socks" was given to me because as a youth I would wear six to eight pairs of socks, various colors folded down so all colors would show. Sometimes I'd wear just the colors to match the colors in my outfits. To fit the eight pairs of socks, I'd buy my shoes and skates in a larger size. I'd wear them mostly roller skating, which is my favorite pastime. I'd also go out dancing and take off my shoes and dance in my socks. To this day, I still wear two to three pairs of socks or leg warmers, color-coordinated to match my outfits when I go roller skating. Throughout the years, I've developed a large skate family and many of them only know me by the name "Socks." My other skate names include Detroit, Auntie, Big Sis, Momma Socks, OG, and Triple OG.

I have been roller skating for sixty years. I loved roller skating from the very beginning and have maintained that love throughout the years.

I first started roller skating around the age of seven on steel outdoor shoe clip-on skates. I skated on the sidewalk in front of my house and up and down the street.

In Detroit, Michigan, where I was born and raised, the roller rink that impacted me the most was The Arcadia Roller Rink. My first indoor roller skating experience around the age of ten was at The Arcadia Roller Rink on Woodward Avenue. My mother would make my older sister, Sharon, take me skating with her. She'd be mad about it, but took me anyway rather than not being able to go herself. My

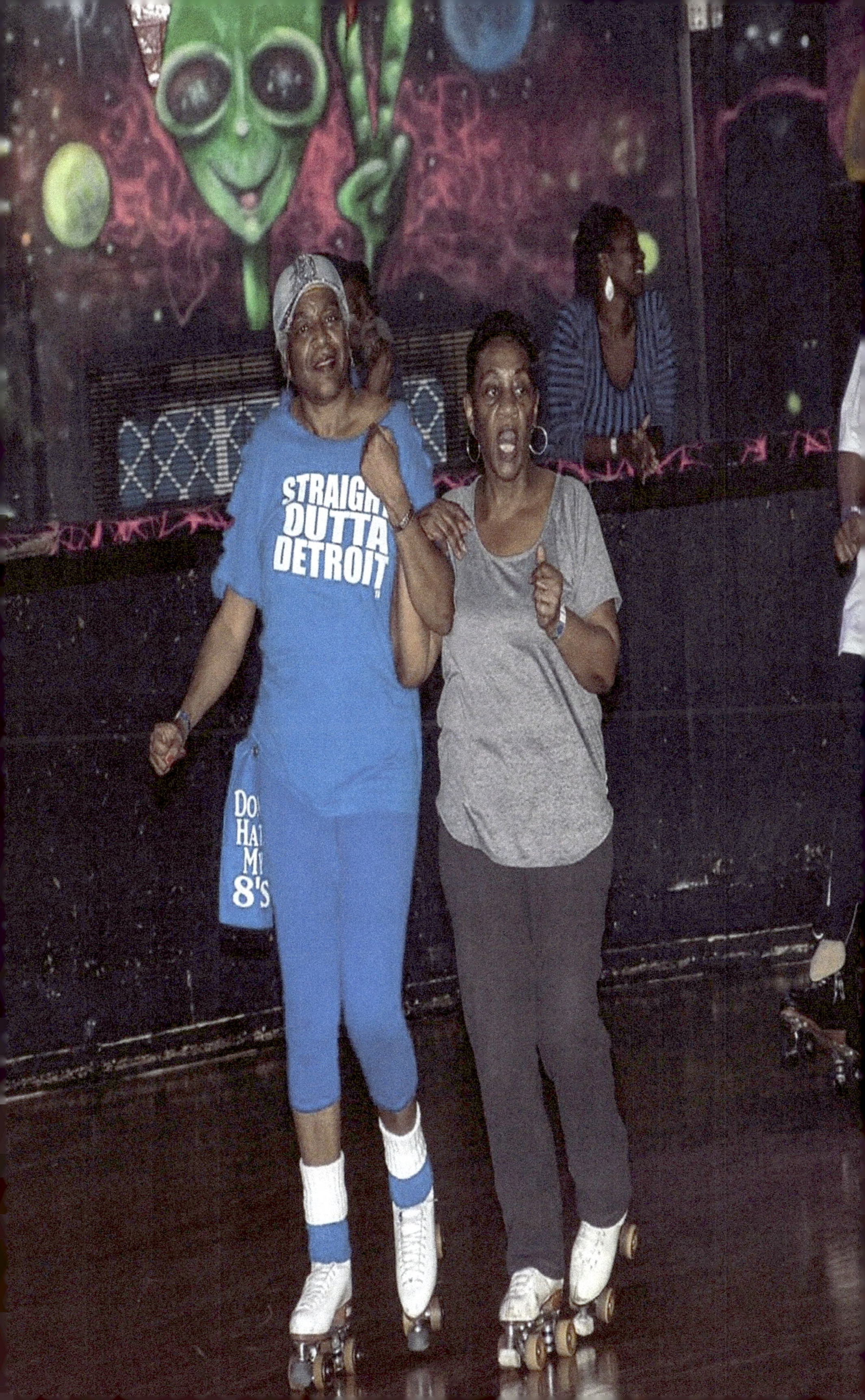
STRAIGHT
OUTTA
DETROIT

mother was also a skater at the Arcadia, so guess you could say…it's in my blood!

I recall my first Arcadia experience as a very frightening one. The skaters had no sympathy for beginners. The word at the rink was "If you get on the floor, you better skate and don't fall or you'll get run over!" I found that to be true by standing on the outside of the skating floor, watching the advanced skaters fly by and those who did fall got their arms, legs, etc. run over. The skaters did not play…they rolled hard! I found that to be true and quickly decided that I'd better practice skating around the training bar on the outside of the rink until I could skate well enough and build up enough courage to go out onto the floor. Once I was able to hold my own and survived roller skating at the Arcadia, not getting run over or getting jumped on and my skates taken from me, I overcame any previous fear and had no fear of skating anywhere.

I enjoyed going roller skating at The Arcadia on the bus with my friends. Sharon has a friend named DiAnn who she would go skating with. DiAnn's sister, Cynthia Jeffries (Travis), also skated. Cynthia and I started going skating together until I left Detroit and moved to California in 1977. I remember back when Cynthia (my first Sk8 Sistah) and I skated every night, seven nights a week, at the various skating rinks in Detroit and the surrounding areas.

I remember going skating in Belleville and always remember skating in Inkster. When all the other rinks were closed, we would go to Inkster because it was open every night. I hear people talk about Inkster and call it The Safari, but I remember rolling there when the name was The Psychedelic Shack. Seems like the majority of the rinks were called by location rather than rink name. We'd say I'm going to Pontiac…I'm going to the Eastside…I'm going to Flint…I'm going to Canton, etc. The only rink I can think of that we called by its proper name is Northland.

My favorite roller skating rink in Michigan and most memorable experiences were at The Rolladium in Waterford Township in Michigan. We called it Pontiac. I skated every Sunday night for years. During the winter, even in snow and bad weather, Pontiac would be packed. As I reflect, I recall Melvin (RIH) playing the music, tiptoeing across the floor, then back to the DJ booth in time to play the next record. I remember back then I had the energy to skate every record and would only get off the floor on men only. And if one of my skate jams came on, I'd get on the floor during men only and roll around once. I skated all the specials...ladies only, trio/foursome, fast couples, slow couples, and backward couples. I will always cherish those memories!

My skate life has enabled me to meet many great skaters and great friends (Skate Family). Cynthia, one of the best to rock the eights, would always get me back skating whenever I'd stop going. Cynthia has shared her talent and passed on her skills by teaching others. Rockin Richard, King of the Drop, was motivated to share The Motown Sound on Wheels by writing a book. He also represented The D by appearing on The Gong Show winning first place. Some of the other skaters that I recall Rollin with during the late sixties and early seventies are Cynthia's husband Mack, her sister Brenda and cousin Christy; Brenda and Peanut; Willie, Nate, Kendra, Sharon, Big James, Glo, Miguele, Aubrey and many many others. Those were my most memorable and most loved skating days.

My favorite style of roller skating that I enjoy seeing is Detroit Style, which is the style I grew up learning and skating. Detroit skaters have many steps (hops/moves) that they do individually, with a partner, or in a trio/foursome. Back in the day, one of the most common hops was the turnaround which has been renamed the half turn. We also were one of the few cities that did the slide. Detroit is known for sliding and the name Open House was given for sliding only. Also, most times you will see Detroit skaters end with a high hop or high kick to finish their move. Being an OG, I can spot the Ole Skool skaters because they roll with their arms up, kicking it out cutting center, which is my favorite move. Many of the younger skaters also roll like that, but it's just something about the old way that stands out to me, probably because I moved away so long ago. I used to do some of the hops, slides, and drops, but for quite a while have lost my ability to roll like I once did.

I never entered any skate contests in Detroit, but was on the "Rolling Funk" roller skating television shows. I was never a member of a skate club in Detroit, but have many friends that belong to skate clubs.

The Detroit Skate Club I am closely tied to is The Detroit Rhythmic Rollers (DRR) who sponsored the very first Roller Skating Cruise coordinated by Theresa Jones (Ms. Tee, RIH). It was an absolutely wonderful experience, rollin' on the ship as we cruised the Caribbean Islands.

When I left Detroit and moved to Los Angeles, California, in 1977, I realized Detroit had its own unique smooth style of roller skating. I was shocked when I walked into a skating rink in California to see that everyone skated differently than what I was used to. At that time I had not done out-of-state roller skating, so had no idea that other states had such different styles of roller skating. I can walk into a rink, look out on the floor and immediately spot a Detroit skater by their stride and skate style.

I immediately noticed that we skated on different beats, me on the upbeat and they on the down beat. I only knew to skate trios with crisscrossed arms holding hands, but they held hands with one hand instead of two, stretched across the floor. I skated backward slow to slow music; they skated backward fast to fast music. I liked skating fast couples; they had no fast couples. I skated frontwards on ladies only. They once allowed frontwards or backward skating on ladies only, but changed it to backward ladies only. Another immediate difference I noticed was that most of the ladies wear black skates instead of white skates, which I thought was the color skates ladies wore. Most skaters in Detroit wear white boot Riedell skates with Fomac wheels, extended toe stops, and a jump bar, but lots of skaters in Cali wear toe plugs or no toe stops at all. Over the years, many Cali skaters switched over from regular skate boots to Stacy Adams shoes mounted on a skate plate with fiberglass wheels. I choose to stick with my Detroit Hometown skating style and skates, although many of the female Detroit skaters have now switched to black skate boots.

Living in California, I've established a West Coast Skate Family and also have a West Coast Detroit/ Michigan Skate Family of skaters who also moved to Cali from Michigan. It didn't take long before I met others from Detroit that moved to California, in both Southern and Northern Cali. The Detroit Skate Family established a skate club named "West Coast Detroiters" and has given skate parties in Northern

Cali and Southern Cali. I was elected President of the Southern Cali West Coast Detroiters and Lawrence Prez Payne was elected President of Northern Cali.

Our West Coast Detroiters Skate Family includes many Michigan skaters, way too many to name individually, but all are loved! I've coordinated on many occasions where we would meet to roll together and what skate shirt to wear as we represented The D! Over the years, I've also become a skate contact for those coming to visit California. I've been told that I'm the glue that holds us together.

My first roller skating experiences living in California were at Venice Beach and Rosecrans Skating Rink.

The Southern California rinks that have impacted my Skate Life are Sherman Square Roller Rink (Reseda); World on Wheels (Los Angeles); Moonlight (Glendale); Skate Depot (Cerritos); Skate Express (Chino); Fountain Valley Skating Center (Fountain Valley); and Skateland Northridge (Northridge). The Northern Cali rinks that I've enjoyed are Cal Skate (Milpitas); The Residence (Home Rink of Fee and Ralph White); Sunrise (Sacramento); and Roller King (Roseville). Skating in California, I've experienced skating among entertainers such as Earth, Wind and Fire; Janet Jackson and other Jackson family members; Anita Baker; and Stevie Wonder, just to name a few.

Living in California allowed me to skate in a couple of movies that featured roller skating...Roller Boogie and Disco Godfather. I practiced to be in the movie Zanadu, however, due to work schedule conflict, I was unable to remain until filming. Although I am not one to enter contests or skate competitively, I was talked into entering a few skate contests. I won a second-place couples trophy in The Coco-Cola Skate Contest skating with Miguele Norwood in Los Angeles and I won a first-place couples trophy skating with Lawrence Payne in Pahrump, Nevada. Our West Coast Detroiters Skate Club has been given lots of recognition as well as being awarded trophies, plaques, awards, and certificates. We won the largest skate group in Arizona for three consecutive years. I guess you could say, I'm one of those behind the scene supporters in the skate world, not interested in being in the spotlight!

I have traveled to roller skate in various states. Those that come to mind are Michigan, Ohio, California, Nevada, Georgia, Florida, Arizona,

Texas, Washington, Maryland, Virginia, Washington, DC, and a few others that I may not recall. I've also roller skated outside the country in Toronto, Canada, and at sea on the Royal Caribbean Cruise Ship.

I've donated skate-related momentums to be displayed to NAARSAP (Roller Skating Archives Project).

During my travels, I have seen many different roller skating styles and various selections of music. Most of the rinks are similar, though my preference is wooden floors. I prefer to roll to R&B, old school, and jazz. I love the music I grew up on, most of it being The Motown Sound. I enjoy music that has a beat that you can feel throughout your body and, as some would say, "skating music" that takes a skater "in their zone" aka into a Sk8 high! If I had to pick one song as my favorite, I'd have to pick "Function at the Junction" by Shorty Long. Back in the day, it was called The Detroit Skater's National Anthem. You would feel the energy on the floor when the song would come on and see groups of skaters hitting the corner in a slide (Open House). "Shot Gun" by Jr. Walker and the Allstars was another popular song during my teenage and early adult life in Detroit. Other old-school favorites include Sugar Hips, Rockin Charlie, several Booker T. and the MGs, and Jr. Walker and the All Stars songs, plus many other instrumental songs. It is my opinion that if you want to see how a certain city or state rolls, go to a regular session, not when there is a big or national skate party. That will allow you to see their real skating style.

In my roller skating experience, I've met and seen skaters of all ages and occupations. Many never know what each other does other than "get their roll on!" Many people are unaware that there is a large population of senior skaters (OGs) that still roll. My opinion is that there is no age limit, too young or too old, for roller skating. I bought my son his first pair of roller skates at two years old.

During my decades of skating, I had never had any major injuries until a few hours before my 67$^{th}$ birthday. I thought I'd be Rollin my birthday in but unfortunately, I had a fall straight back on my head and back. After being helped up, I finished the song in pain then got off the floor and passed out twice. Paramedics said my vitals were good, so I waited until I returned home to see a doctor. My results were that I had fractured ribs and a concussion. A few weeks later, thank God, I was back on my eights.

A lot has changed in roller skating throughout the years. Many rinks have closed and are still closing while some new rinks have opened. The new generations have brought new vibes, styles, and new music, but the culture is still one of love and passion. Roller skating has had a great impact on my life and remains my favorite pastime. It is great exercise, a way to release stress (leave it on the wood), a means of establishing lifelong friendships and partnerships, entertaining, and has given me the most enjoyable memories of my life!

I believe roller skating will be around forever! It's a skate thing you just don't understand unless you are a skater! I love to skate and will continue to *get my roll on* until the wheels and legs fall off!

Roller skating has truly been a blessing from God!

Many thanks to God for blessing me with a long, joyful skate journey. Thanks to Queen Amirah and staff for their dedication to putting our skate life experiences in print to share with others. Thanks to Ice and Rockin Richard for believing my story is worth telling, and thanks to everyone else for allowing me to reminisce and share a bit of my skate history, love, and passion. Let's roll…

*Do You Know...*

## Roller Skating Diplomacy

During the height of the Cold War in 1971, roller skating took on an unexpected role in international diplomacy with the journey of a group of American roller skaters dubbed the "Roller Skating Diplomats." As part of a cultural exchange program between the United States and China, these skaters traveled to China to promote goodwill and understanding. Roller skating served as a common ground for interaction and communication, breaking down barriers and fostering mutual understanding between people from different backgrounds. Through exhibitions, demonstrations, and friendly competitions, the Roller Skating Diplomats showcased the joy and camaraderie that roller skating can bring, leaving a lasting impression on their Chinese counterparts.

The visit of the Roller Skating Diplomats to China was met with curiosity and enthusiasm from both sides, transcending political tensions and promoting friendship through sport. Their efforts helped to humanize international relations and build bridges of understanding between nations, highlighting the power of sports diplomacy to transcend political divides and promote peace. By using roller skating as a tool for cultural exchange, the Roller Skating Diplomats made a meaningful contribution to improving relations between the United States and China, leaving a legacy of friendship that endures to this day.

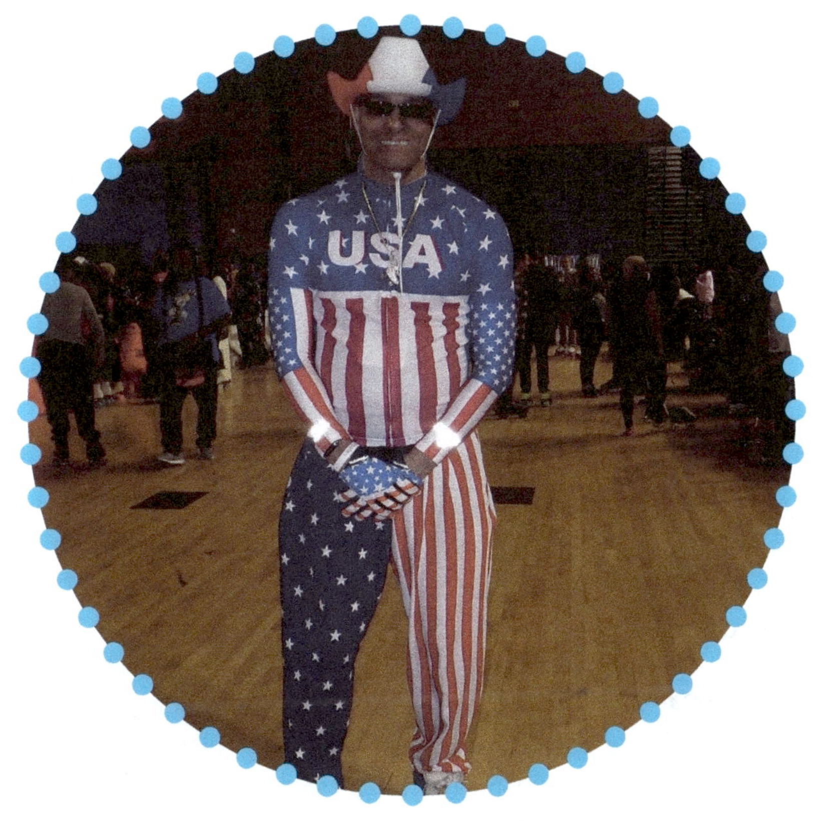


Touré Clark

aka Uncle Jamm

Faacebook: @Toure Clark :| Instagram @unclejamm1959

# "My Roller Skating Career"

The first time I put on roller skates was in Berkeley, California, in the 1960s and got to see Richard Humphrey and fellow skaters in Golden Gate Park, San Francisco, California, in the 1970s. When I was in elementary and in the school's library, I saw the book Jammin Art to Roller Skating by Bill Butler. When I lived in Washington, DC, my ex-wife took me to the Alexandra Roller Dome in Alexandra, Virginia (1983) and I was reintroduced to skating. When I joined the Marine Corps in 1984 and got assigned to Okinawa, Japan, and Camp Kinser with 3rd FSSG, I discovered the skating rink NAHA ROLLER that was only a mile from my installation. That's where I got to learn the art of jam skating in the Far East.

From 1984 to 1985 and 1987 to 1988, I spent most of my time skating and learning until my change of duty to Camp Lejeune in Jacksonville, North Carolina. While in Jacksonville, there was one local skating rink called SKATE WORLD (1985-1987). Every Friday night and Saturday the rink would be packed with military and their dependents and locals. On Sunday night the adult session was at the Galaxy of Sports in Kinston, North Carolina, with DJ MAGIC. In the 1980s, I would travel to different skating rinks and meet and greet different skaters and their styles. After my eight years in the Marine Corps (1984-1992), I moved to Southern Georgia and lived in the Americus, Plains Georgia area (1992-1995), and went skating in Albany, Georgia, at Stardust and in the Macon, Georgia area. In 1995, I returned to the Craven County area and back to the Galaxy of Sports in Kinston, North Carolina. I started coming to Raleigh, North

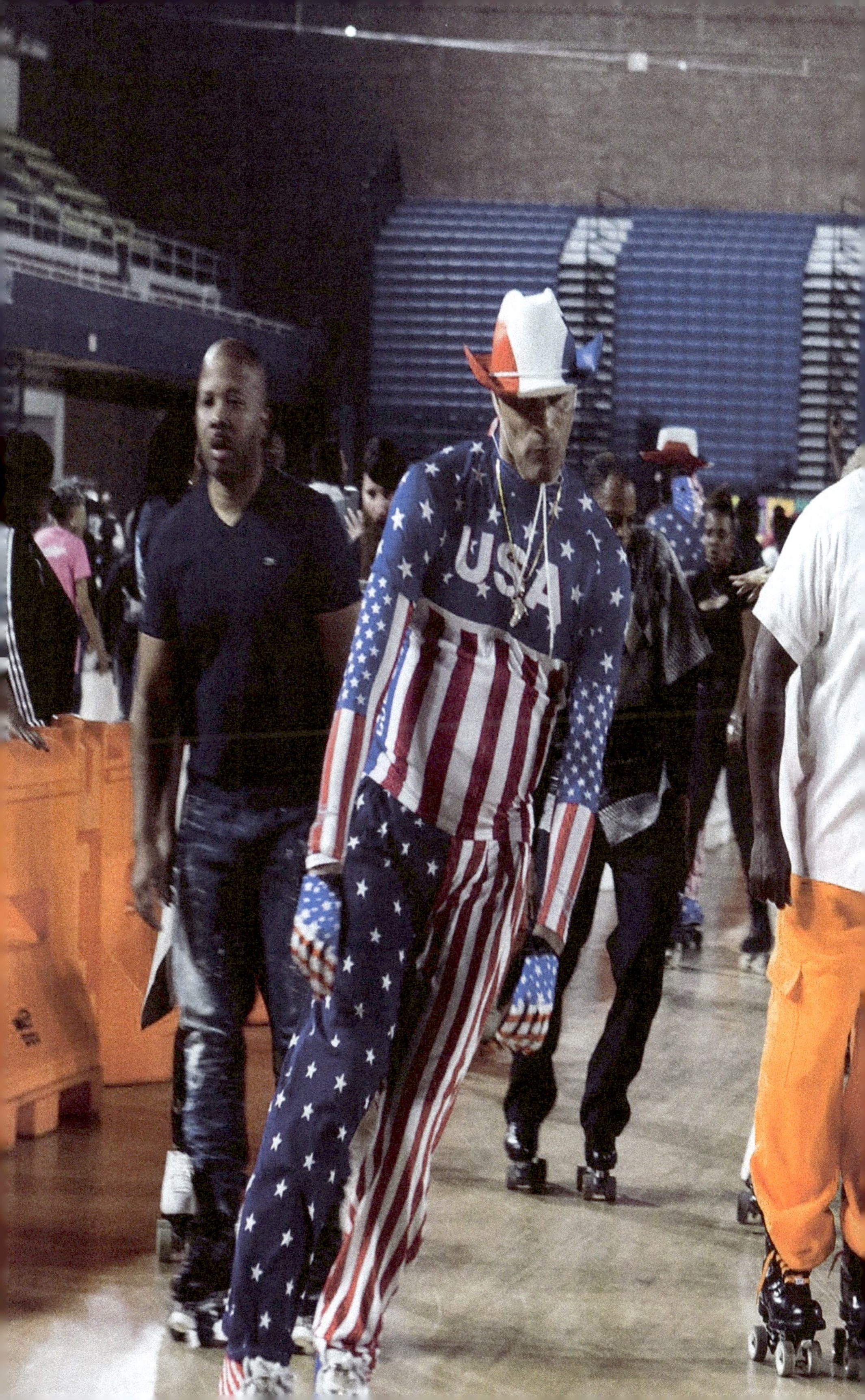
USA

Carolina, and Skate Ranch on Sunday Night and reunited with many of the skaters from the Galaxy of Sports.

The first time I heard about SK8-A-THON held in Virginia was from Chris Gaddy. After attending that event, he introduced me to Rolling in the Carolinas Event and I was hooked. When I got called to active duty in 2003 and assigned to Fort Jackson, South Carolina, from 2003 to 2007, I went skating at the local rink called Redwing Rollerway on Decker Boulevard. This skating rink was the heartbeat of the Columbia area with skaters coming from Atlanta, North Carolina, and the surrounding area to roll to the awesome mixes by DJ SWAGG. I would travel to Augusta and skate at Redwing Rollerway or pass through Atlanta and skate at the Golden Glide. When Redwing Rollerway was closed because of poor management, the only place for adult skaters to roll was in Charlotte, North Carolina at Kate's. The DJ/skater, Barry White, asked the co-owners, the Phillips family, about having a Sunday night adult session and the rest is history!

So after my many years of skating and becoming the first soldier to create and perform for the U.S. Army with the 2009 U.S. Army Soldier Show, I am honored to have gotten the chance to audition for America's Got Talent (4X) and give back to my military community at Fort Jackson, South Carolina, and across the USA and overseas. After my many years of Skating, sadly I had to put my skates on the shelf until I return to 100% because of having two total hip replacement surgeries in 2017!

Now, I am sixty-two years old, fully recovered, and proud to have had the great opportunity to showcase my God-given talent with my own style. You can see me on YouTube (@UncleJamm49) and see why my motto is, "It's never about me, but what is in front of me that counts!"

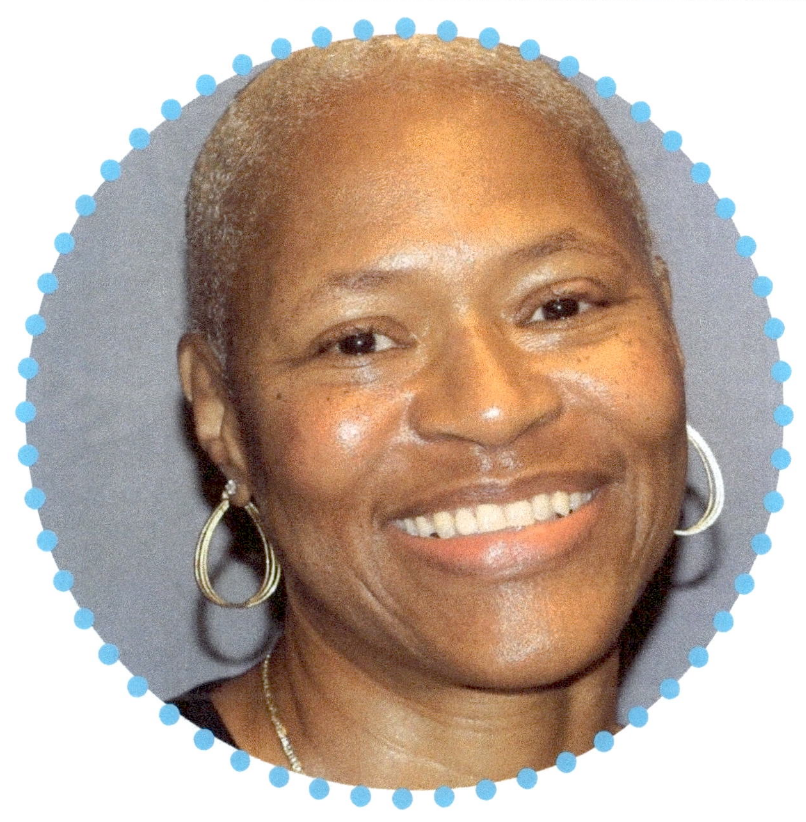

## Myra Muhammad

Facebook: @Myra Muhammad | Instagram: @sixfigures2022

# "I Leave My Stress on the Wood."

My parents introduced me to skating. They both skated and, in my eyes, my dad was the smoothest skater on Earth. Skating was a family event. My aunties, uncles, cousins all skated, and we continued to skate together for many years. My mom put me on skates at age seven. I can still remember going to Twin City Skating Rink in Elizabeth, New Jersey, on Friday nights with my parents and Saturday with my sister and cousins. On Saturdays, they would have races at the rink to see which kid was the fastest skater. My cousins and I always looked forward to the races.

As a young teen, my parents no longer skated, so it was my sister and cousins that made it a Saturday night event. By this time, there was no longer organ music but records being played and the party at the rink was electric. We always stayed until the end of the session, knowing that the last bus home would come soon and if we missed it, we had a long walk home. Knowing this, we did it anyway and everyone would run for that last bus.

As my cousins and I got older and Twin City began doing late-night adult sessions, we could not wait to get to the rink. Seeing all the great skaters and different styles; we were always trying to learn something new each week.

Once Twin City closed, I stopped skating for a while until my mom took me to Skate 22 in Union, New Jersey. A much smaller rink, but the energy was everything. I was not totally back to skating yet, but always had a great time when I went. Once I had my son, I put him on skates at the tender age of two; he enjoyed our time together at the

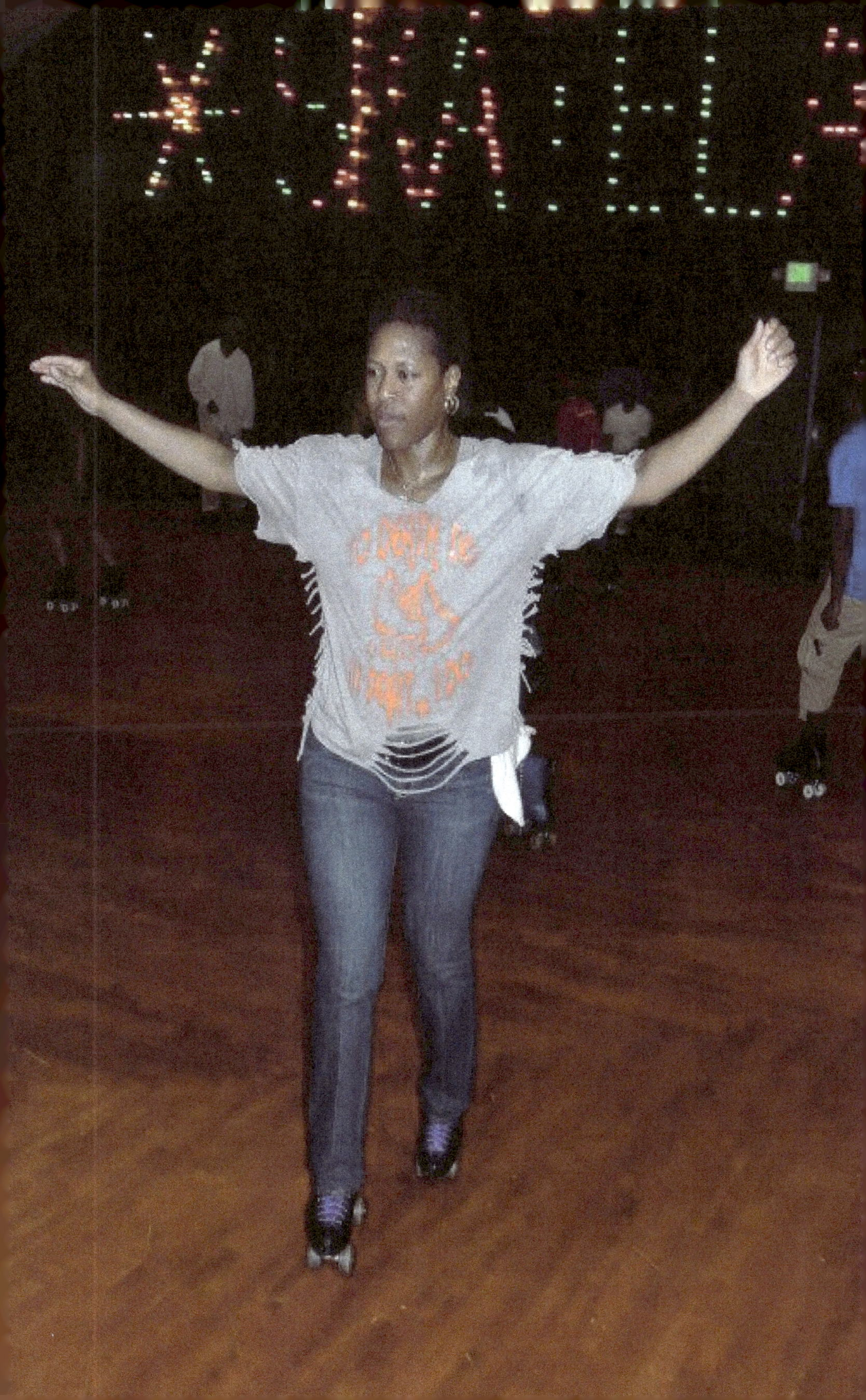

rink but unfortunately, he did not have a love for skating like me. My sisters and cousins stopped skating, and I began to skate at USA roller rink in Edison, New Jersey. I made some friends at USA and began skating the adult session on Sunday nights until they closed. A friend told me that everyone was now skating at Skate 22 on Wednesday nights, and I made my way there and it was much closer to my house.

Skate 22 became my home. There were many familiar faces from Twin City and USA. I developed beautiful friendships and picked up a few mentors at the rink. My love for skating grew deeper and all I could think about was being on the wood on Wednesday nights with my skate family. I began bringing my nephew skating on Friday nights family sessions and that's where I met Anthony. He skated on Friday nights with his two sons. Anthony did line skating, developed all these skate moves, and I wanted to learn. So, on Friday nights he would teach me, Marsha, Akili, and Joe skate moves, and on Wednesday nights we would do our moves. One night, Anthony came to the rink with t-shirts for us to wear when we skated on Wednesday and Friday nights, and Heaven on Wheels (H.O.W.) was created.

Anthony taught us close to one hundred different steps and he would be on us until we got it right. On Friday nights during the family session, parents would always comment on how great we looked doing our steps. Many of the children would try to learn them, but some of the moves were intricate. It would sometimes take us all night to get a move right. It was my job to learn the moves from Anthony and teach the rest of the group.

I began traveling with other skaters to different skate parties and it was always nice when people would come up to me and ask, "Is your group with you? Are you guys doing your steps tonight?" H.O.W. developed as a family and still is to this day. Skate 22 was home for Heaven on Wheels, and we welcomed anyone wanting to learn.

In December 2008, Skate 22 was closed for a period. The skate community rallied together to get the rink open again. It reopened in May 2009. During this time, a new skate group was formed with a few veteran skaters. The group was called Many Issues Concerning Skaters (M.I.C.S.), of which I was a founding member. We worked to keep the rink free from people with the agenda of starting trouble. One thing we worked very hard at was creating a family environment, trying to bring back some of what we all had as children. Parents enjoying time with family and friends at the rink. We felt it was important for children to see this relationship; parents and children enjoying clean fun together. So M.I.C.S., with the approval of the rink owner, Phil, started doing children skate parties. Our first party was a Halloween party from 11 am to 11 pm. We asked DJs to donate their time for the event and all the DJs were more than willing to do so. The rink owner donated a pair of skates along with Skillz & Skates, all the members of M.I.C.S. and H.O.W. donated candy, my mom would make spaghetti in a turkey sauce, and a skater from Maryland would always donate gift cards for our events and we had a full twelve-hour party. All non-skating parents would get in free; we wanted the parents to be a part of this event. We created skate games for the children to play; we did costume contests, fed the families, and gave each kid candy as they left the rink. The only thing a parent needed to do when they got home was to bathe the children and put them to bed. We did two to three parties a year, each with a different theme: like Rolling Back to School, where we gave out school supplies to the children, and Rolling into Fitness, where we had fitness instructors come out and talk about the importance of health. We gave away three-month memberships to a gym. The back-to-school skate parties were a huge success. The children and parents were thrilled with the gifts they received. We were fortunate to have people and some vendors willing to donate to our events. The second year of M.I.C.S began a collaboration with H.O.W. and joined forces to continue these very successful parties. After the second or third year, H.O.W. took over doing the parties on their own. The children and parents looked forward to the annual Halloween party. Some of the costumes were over the top, but we enjoyed doing these events for the children.

Skate 22 closed in 2015, which was a sad day for us all. We never knew the importance of these events until the closing of Skate 22. Parents and children expressed how much they looked forward to our parties every year and thanked us for giving them the opportunity to experience something so amazing. Skating allowed H.O.W. the opportunity to bring people together, and we were grateful for the opportunity. Watching this generation grow up in the rink and now seeing young adults, and how they still enjoy skating. Most have grown into excellent skaters and are teaching others.

H.O.W. now skates at Branch Brook Park roller rink in Newark, New Jersey. We can no longer do our twelve-hour skate events, but we continue to give back with our annual coat/toy drive. We donate all coats to the Salvation Army and donate toys to the Division of Youth and Family Services.

I love going skating. I'm able to leave my stressful day on the wood and that's always a good feeling. I have made so many great friendships and some sisters "from another mother." The bond that I've developed with my skate family is so important to me. I work with some amazing people in and out of the rink.

H.O.W. is still going strong. We are still learning new moves—some more intricate than others. Some faces have changed, but we are still a family. We still look forward to passing the torch when that day comes, but for now, we will continue to do what we do best and that is steppin'.

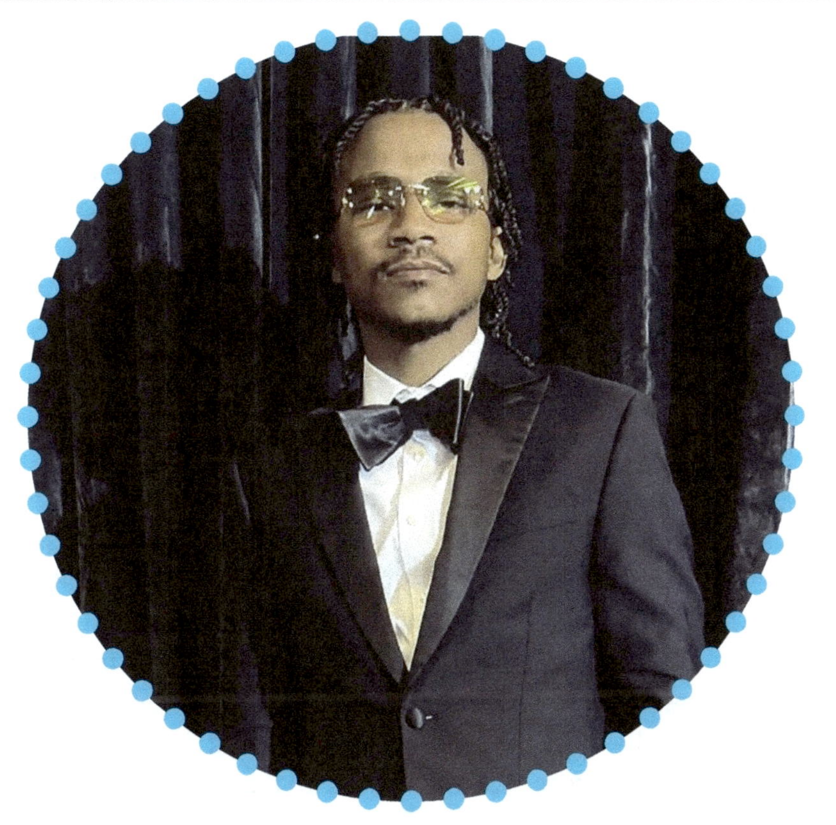

Victor Smith

Facebook: @Victor Smith | Instagram: @realsince94

## "The art of skating will continue to evolve over the years."

If I don't have anything in the world I have skating. Skating is my all-in-one, something like love at first sight. One of the things in life I'll never let go of, no matter what. I still remember my first pair of Chicago skates—black boot with blue wheels, heavy metal plate with the balance bar. Growing up, I had other hobbies such as playing basketball, riding and fixing my bikes, and many other things, but nothing brought the feeling that skating brought. How some people do well in basketball or any other sports, that's skating for me. Skating is my gift. Skating is a keepsake to me, from all the memories and bonds I've built with people.

In 2018, a few people and I started our skate group called SOLID8's. Looking even further going back to my family, most of us skated. We had reunions at Orchard Skateland located in the northeast part of Baltimore. That's where the passion began. I would look forward to going to our family skate party every year. I looked up to my older cousins. That made me want to be the best I could be at skating. As a kid, birthday skate parties and regular sessions every weekend were the highlights of my week. Friday nights at Orchard back when I was in middle school— those were the good days. When Orchard closed back in 2014, it impacted many people because people grew up skating there. I know for a fact that the Orchard will always hold a piece of my heart, because that's where it all started. I still remember my first Scenario skate party in 2013. That was a skate party to remember. It was a bitter-sweet moment because that was the last time the Scenario

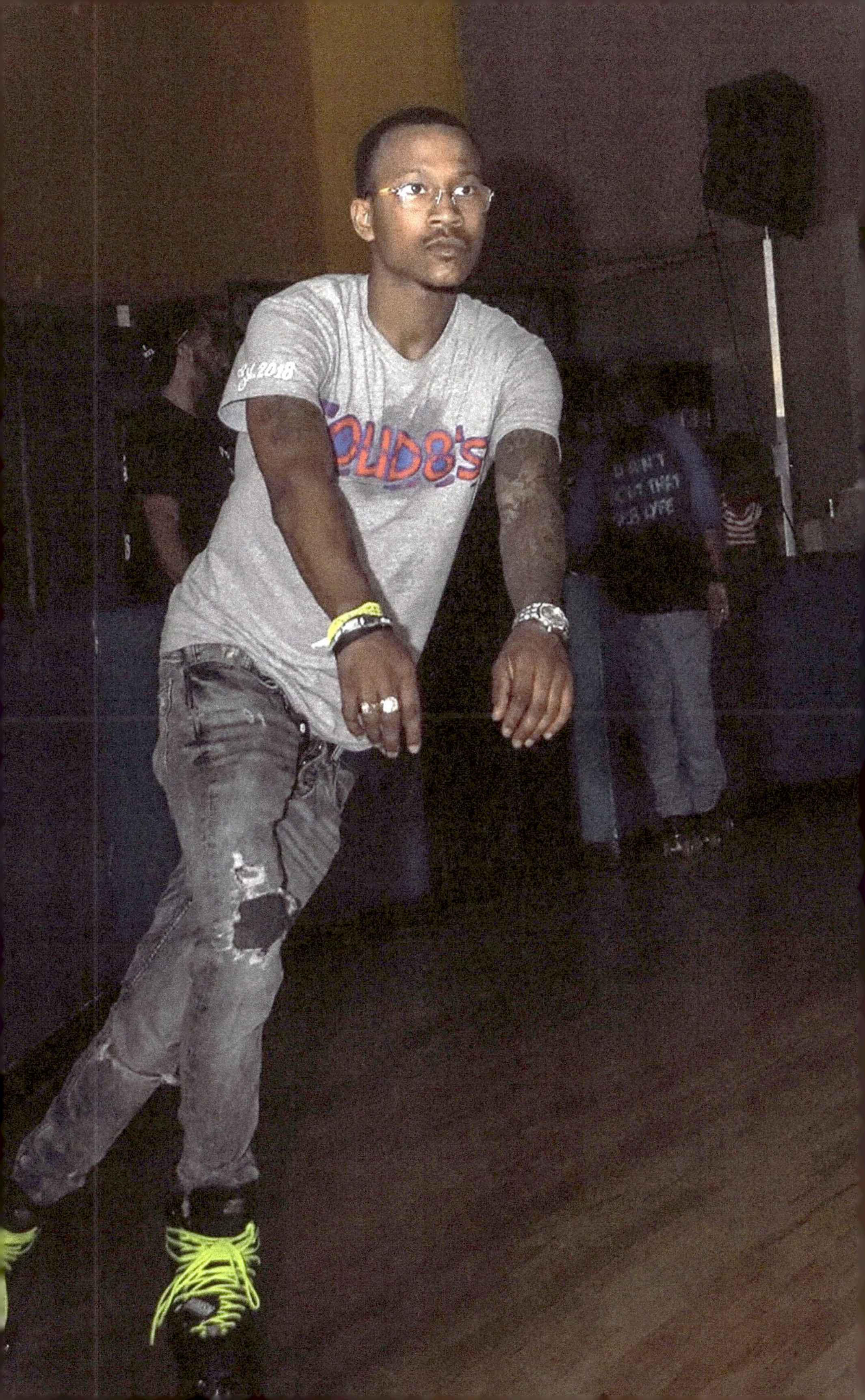

skate party was held. At least I got the chance to attend at least one of them. If it were up to me, Orchard would still be open.

The art of skating will continue to evolve over the years. I'm glad I'll be a part of it, inspiring and motivating people to skate and also to be better at skating. Skating had taught me a lot about myself. Skating showed I can do whatever I put my mind to. Skating helped boost my confidence and trust within, while also improving my coordination. Skating taught me a great amount of patience. I have applied skills I acquired from skating to driving and when I ride my dirt bike. Knowing how far I've come as a skater drives me to keep getting better while also learning new styles. Pushing myself and testing my limits; I never tell myself that I "can't" do something. When I put my skates on, my skates and I become one. The preciseness of catching every beat and the different combinations of moves is like drawing art. Or cooking on an open fire; it takes a special type of finesse. Once I lock in I'm like a lion hunting a gazelle. To see the different angles when choosing my path of direction makes a difference.

I consider myself a versatile skater. Snapping has influenced my skate style. Here in Baltimore our home style of skating is called "snapping," which we share with skaters from Washington, D.C.. Together we call it "Snap City." Snapping was the first skate style that I learned. I first learned basic snap moves. I learned snapping to the left, snapping to the right. While going frontwards and while backward and also turning to the inside and the outside. Once I got comfortable with the basic maneuvers, I started being creative by adding my own style to snapping. I always wanted to look different, do the moves differently than everyone else. That's what makes me unique. While snapping, I aim to hit every beat on the beat I'm skating to. The adrenaline rush from cutting the middle and playing in traffic is unexplainable. Cutting the middle is like a big figure 8 instead of going in the traditional direction. It looks so smooth when it's done correctly. Playing in traffic is skating in the opposite direction, slow and under control. Going from inside to the outside is a freestyle of skating while avoiding people and grooving to the beat of the music. It might sound crazy, but it's a ton of fun. Fast backward was the next style of skating that I learned. I first saw it at Millennium Skate World in Camden, New Jersey, on a first Wednesday. First Wednesday is a skate party that happens on the first Wednesday of every month. Even though it took me a few times to get comfortable doing fast backward, I was persistent and determined to learn fast backward. My thing was skating so close to the wall, going so fast backward at that. Once I got the hang of it, it became second nature to me. Now I don't worry about the wall or falling. I just let the music and my momentum carry me. When I'm doing fast backward, it feels like I'm floating on air. I'm constantly thinking of ways to make my snap and freestyle moves look smoother and swifter, while also thinking of new moves to try. I tell myself to keep calm and don't panic. That gives me better reaction time. Especially if someone is next to me or if they are falling. I already have another path of direction in sight. Things happen so fast, as an experienced skater, I feel responsible if someone falls because I went past them.

Skating keeps me out of trouble, and it also saved my life. Once I realized I took being able to actually go skating for granted, it made me more dedicated and love skating even more. Having an outlet such as skating is amazing. Traveling to different cities and meeting new people, while trying new food; I appreciate skating because some people don't have the same outlet or an outlet at all. To have something you can call your own, something to make you happy when you're down or just having a bad day, is important. Skating two times out of the week helps me clear my mind. I feel free when I'm skating, nothing matters. Whatever was on my mind before doesn't matter once I get on the skate floor. The music just carries me. It's something about the bass when it's knocking. You can hear it from outside of the rink. Honestly, I couldn't picture my life without skating. I would feel incomplete. If I don't attend my weekly skate sessions, I feel off because I know I won't be able to decompress my thoughts until the following week. I treat skating with a delicacy like the finest caviar. I'm forever grateful to be blessed with a gift such as skating.

*Do You Know...*

## Roller Skating Outdoors

Outdoor roller skating offers skaters a refreshing way to enjoy the sport while connecting with nature and exploring their surroundings. Unlike indoor rinks, outdoor skating allows skaters to experience a variety of terrain and scenery, from smooth sidewalks to scenic trails. Skating outdoors provides a sense of freedom and liberation, allowing skaters to enjoy fresh air and sunshine while gliding through open spaces.

When skating outdoors, it's important to choose suitable locations with smooth and even surfaces to minimize the risk of falls or injuries. Sidewalks, paved bike paths, and designated skating trails are ideal for outdoor roller skating, providing ample space for safe maneuvering. Urban landscapes and parks offer diverse settings for skating, whether skaters prefer bustling city streets or serene natural environments.

Outdoor roller skating can be enjoyed solo or with friends and family, making it a social and recreational activity. Many skaters organize group outings, meetups, or participate in organized skating events and tours. Skating outdoors allows skaters to discover new routes, explore different neighborhoods, and share the joys of roller skating while basking in the beauty of the great outdoors.

Overall, outdoor roller skating provides a refreshing alternative to indoor rink skating, offering skaters an invigorating experience that combines physical activity with exploration and adventure. Whether skating through city streets or gliding along scenic trails, outdoor skating allows skaters to embrace the freedom of movement, connect with nature, and enjoy the simple pleasure of rolling under the open sky.

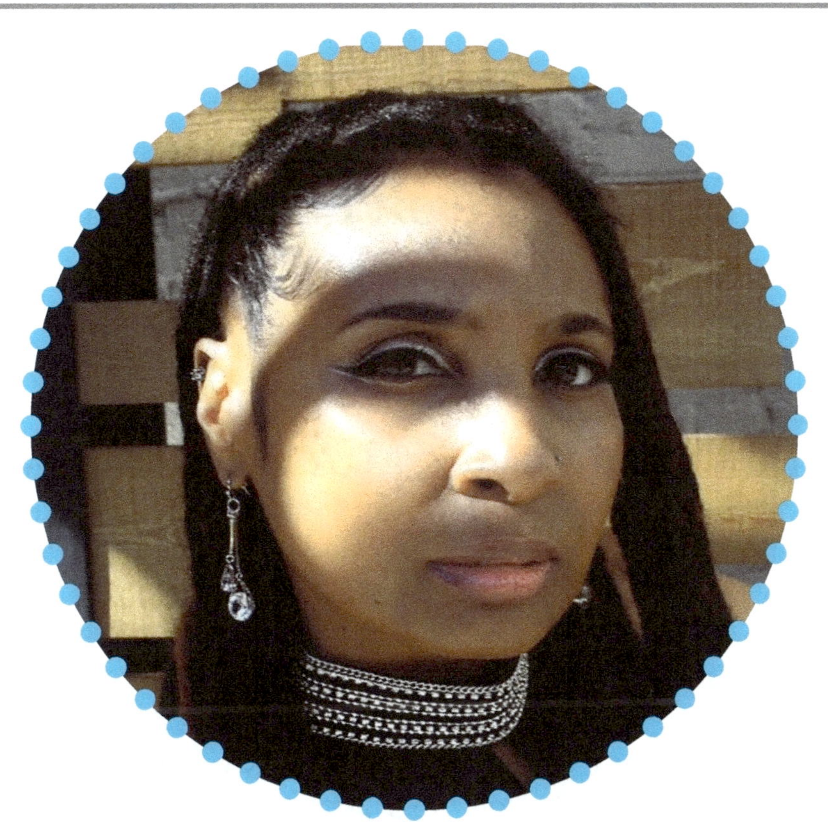

April Guillory

aka Mz. Black Diamond

Facebook: @April Blackdiamond
Instagram: @mz-blackdiamond

# "Finding Peace on Eight Wheels"

When I think about my journey in the skate community, it brings overwhelming joy to my spirit, giving me a sense of relief and peace from my everyday life of responsibilities. Skating creates moments where I can just be a free spirit living in a chaotic world. This environment is an escape from everyday life and for me becomes a phenomenal feeling I can't express in words. To encourage as well as be inspired by others creates a surge of emotions beyond explanation. To see people of different nationalities and gender come together for the love of one hobby is life-changing. In the presence of the true essence of skating you learn life's lessons from a close-knit community—friendships, breakups, love, hate, birth, loss, success, rebuilding, and the list goes on yet one of the most important lessons is UNITY. During hard times, having the ability to come together and support your fellow man like family with love is always a refreshing moment. It's also shown when dire circumstances occur, which makes it even more beautiful to witness the camaraderie.

Now the first day of my recollection falling in love with skating goes back to my childhood from six to eight years old while growing up in Mobile, Alabama. I still remember that day. Awakened by my mom while in my pajamas, she asked, "Would you like to go with me and your auntie?" Of course, I said yes. Who wouldn't want to go on a late-night adventure (at least around that age I thought

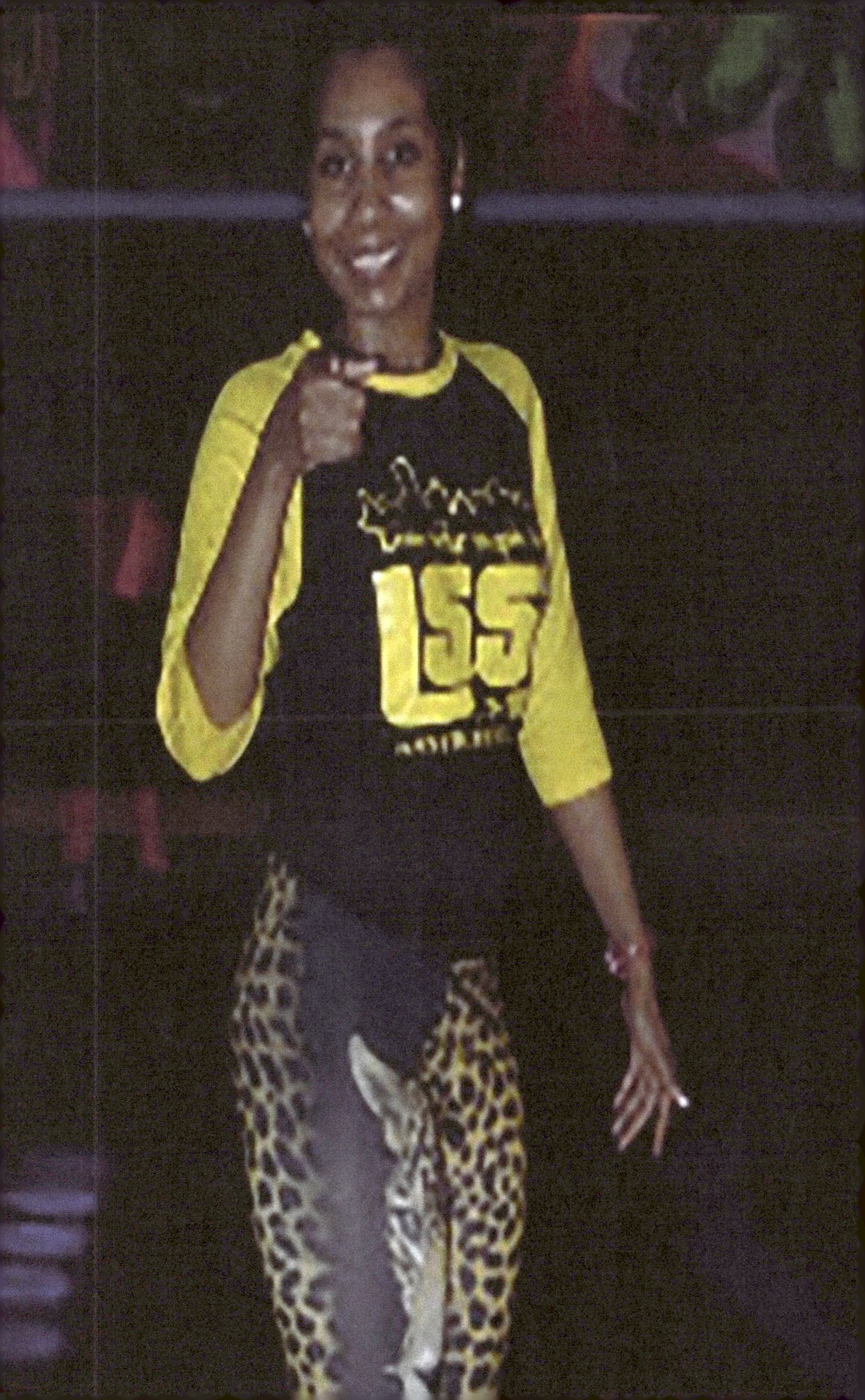

it was late) with your family? As she took my hand, I thought to myself, *I'm a big girl now because I get to stay up late with my mom and auntie.* As we traveled to this mysterious place, I fell asleep in the back of her vehicle and, to my surprise, woke up to this building with a lot of people. I wondered to myself, *What's going on and why I'm here in my pajamas?* Entering the building, I became amazed, witnessing the display of people, lights, and sounds in front of me. I witnessed people of all ages from teens to adults rolling around in a huge circle performing incredible tricks on skates. They seemed to move effortlessly around the hardwood floor. I became so mesmerized by the different moves, styles, and synchronisms witnessed that night and found myself moving as close as I could get to the floor without interrupting the show. I thought to myself, *Is this what adults/teenagers do at night? I want to be an adult/teenager now!* As much as I wanted to get out there with them, I wasn't content with just watching. The lights were beautiful and seemed to dance on the skate floor with the people. I recall seeing male skaters doing tricks which made me blush, but now that I'm older and more aware, I now know they were just trying to impress my mom and auntie (yeah make the child smile to get next to the female(s) trick lol). I still enjoyed the performance, as I stayed close to my family. My biggest joy throughout that night was watching my family skate. To me, they looked like superheroes on wheels, and I wanted to be just like them.

While my mom worked the following day, I went into her closet and took her skates. Going into the kitchen, I was determined to learn how to skate just like my family members. Of course, the skates were too big, and I ended up busting my behind, but I didn't give up and through my own focus and determination, I'm a self-taught roller skater. Over a period-of-time, I learned to balance, move forward and backward, and turn while in my mom's oversized skates. She never knew I was secretly taking her skates and learning in the kitchen. When she finally realized what I was doing with her skates, she seemed impressed that I was self-taught.

When the holidays came around, she asked, "What do you want for Christmas?" I stated, "Skates," but I should have been more specific. As the holiday arrived, I became excited to open my gift. However, to my surprise, I got what I asked for. Unfortunately, they were inline skates. I wanted quad skates. I saw the excitement on my mom's face when she saw me open the gift. She even got them in my favorite color, purple. I thanked her for my gift and gave her the biggest hug I could muster because I knew she tried her best to make my Christmas special and we didn't have a lot. As I put the inline skates on, I'll tell you, I looked extremely crazy in them. I couldn't keep my balance to save my life. It felt so uncomfortable. I continued skating with them for a little while, eventually letting skating go because I didn't want to seem ungrateful. Years passed and as life continued to move forward and I had a family of my own, it was at that moment I decided to renew the passion that never left my heart. Laying dormant in my spirit, I rekindled my love for the skating rink's floor/wood.

Living in Newport News, Virginia, I searched diligently and found a rink nearby with a family session, and it was like I was a kid all over again. The fun was unreal. Yet again, I became mesmerized by the skills and unique styles of different skaters in an atmosphere where my spirit had desperately missed. Little did I know my family, and I were in one of the melting pots for skating because of the city having a military base nearby. We were able to view styles from north, south, east, west, and in-between. As my passion for skating grew even stronger, I decided to invest in my own pair of skates. Thinking that I should get something like tennis shoes, my first pair were jam skates (lol).... I learned these skates don't give the best ankle support. When I was ready to really learn how to skate like the "professionals," I learned my first lesson on "skate politics"—not everyone is willing to teach you. I decided to continue to teach myself, admiring the skating styles of the men, not the women, and wanted to move similar yet with a female touch. A kind man named Tommy Hill, who mentored me on the fundamentals of skating, came into my life during a time when I really needed help. His style was JB (James Brown/Chicago based). I felt so honored and pleased that someone noticed how hard I was trying and wanted to help. Another lesson learned: Don't be too big within yourself to help others. As time progressed and my skills got sharper, then I noticed once that happened other people decided to help me even further, which I was appreciative. I'm still grateful for the kindness Tommy Hill displayed because you never know what a simple act of kindness will do for a person.

In 2010, my family moved to Dallas/Fort Worth, Texas, which is now my current home. When moving here, I immediately searched for a skating rink in my local area to ensure the continuation of my skate journey. I finally found a local rink that played Hip Hop and R&B with an adult session. I came across Forum Skating Rink. Due to some of the encounters from the previous rink in Virginia, I decided to first observe the behavior of the locals and, as time progressed, I noticed some of the familiar styles I learned from Virginia on display. To my surprise, most of the people were very hospitable, so I started interacting more with those in the rink and I also recall some people even mentioning "What took you so long to say anything?" I told my story, and they understood. Lesson: Don't let the encounters from the past interrupt the possibilities of the present." As time progressed, I've created wonderful friendships, and even became a member of a skate group called "Texas Outlawz." We flowed by our own rules and had a hilarious time just making people happy. Participating in various skating events and showcasing our talents, yet most importantly, demonstrating genuine hospitality and fun wherever we visit was our main thing. Always showing respect to other cities within the skate community allows everyone a chance to share different styles and history in appreciation with other locations. It's truly a learning experience to receive the skate community knowledge of the deeply rooted history. The "Texas Outlawz" has grown and evolved over the years, but we still have the love for the group in our hearts, as well as the memories to back it up. Lesson: "Family isn't always blood-related and because things change doesn't mean the love doesn't remain."

Currently, I've been noticed for the "Slow Walk" skate style, which showcases a free flow of movements I bring while skating. "Slow Walk" became popular and was created by "Mr. Slow Walk" from Louisville, Kentucky. People noticed my updated style of the Slow Walk and deemed me as "Slow Walk Queen." My style is just that, My Style (being a free spirit) and I take no ownership in the original creation. However, I am honored by the people that deem me as the "Slow Walk Queen." Receiving the acknowledgment and approval from "Mr. Slow Walk" was an honor as well. I've always loved to dance, and my style allows my body to flow with the music and enjoy the moments in time. My status in the skate community is just being a positive representation of myself. To make sure other people are comfortable within my presence, so I can be an example of skate unity, always staying mindful of my prior challenges in the skate community because of previous encounters where there was a lack of help and support. We all had to start somewhere, so why not help your fellow man and build a stronger skate community.

# Do You Know...

## Roller Skating Ettiquette

Roller skating etiquette is essential for fostering a positive and enjoyable experience for everyone at the rink. Being mindful of other skaters is paramount; always be aware of your surroundings and avoid sudden stops or erratic movements that could pose a hazard to yourself and others. Maintaining control of your speed and direction is crucial for safety, especially in crowded rink environments where collisions can occur if skaters aren't attentive.

Additionally, following any rules or guidelines set by the rink staff is essential for ensuring a smooth and harmonious skating session. These rules may include guidelines for entering and exiting the rink, skating in designated areas, and respecting the rights of other skaters. By adhering to these rules, skaters can contribute to a respectful and inclusive atmosphere where everyone can enjoy the sport safely.

Part of roller skating etiquette involves being courteous and considerate to fellow skaters, particularly during busy skating sessions. Yielding the right of way to faster skaters or those practicing routines can help prevent accidents and maintain a fluid skating flow. Likewise, offering assistance or encouragement to novice skaters can foster a supportive and welcoming environment for skaters of all skill levels.

Finally, communication plays a crucial role in roller skating etiquette. If you need to pass another skater or change direction, signaling your intentions with hand gestures or verbal cues can help prevent misunderstandings and promote smooth transitions on the rink. Similarly, being receptive to feedback and respectful of others' space and boundaries contributes to a positive and cooperative skating community.

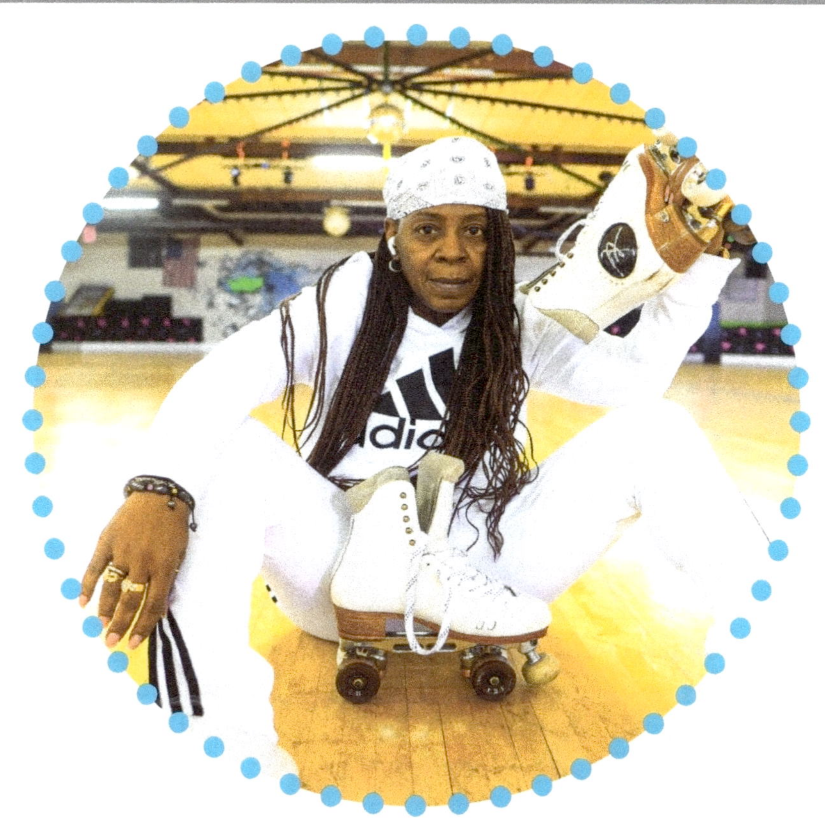


Angie McClendon

Facebook: @Angie McClendon | Instagram: @angiemaccccc

# "Just Skate"

One hot afternoon in Chicago, Illinois, was when my roller-skating life started at five years old. Family members introduced me to roller skating. They took me to a church basement skate session for the first time. My first pair of skates were the kind that had a metal plate; you had to strap them up with your shoes on.

I could not tell everyone my secret, that the skates were too small, and my feet felt like they were in a tuna can. I soon forgot all about that pain, which quickly turned into a ball of breathless excitement, and then I froze. Seeing those people skating, as their feet and bodies had such a rhythmic motion, moving with every beat, like dancing. I was so mesmerized and confused by what I saw, but I knew I wanted to be a roller skater. I saw people skating to the soulful sounds of the music that seemed to resonate throughout their bodies. This was the beginning of my journey to "JUST SKATE."

My family moved to Flint, Michigan. Moving to Flint resurrected my dreams of becoming a skater because it was a small city that thrived around skating, music, sports, and the three-c's: cash, clothes, and cars.

In Flint, all the elementary schools offered roller skating as an after-school activity, which allowed me to skate and make new friends outside of my neighborhood. Even while playing basketball, band ensemble, and karate, my skating progressed, and through that, my popularity as well, and I formed my first skating group. We practiced anywhere we could indoors because we thought it was taboo to skate outside. We didn't want to mess our skates up, which was a huge sign of disrespect back then towards your mom because she worked so hard to get the skates!!! Soon after we heard about a Roller-Skating show called Rolling Funk out of Detroit, Michigan. Fortunately, there was one

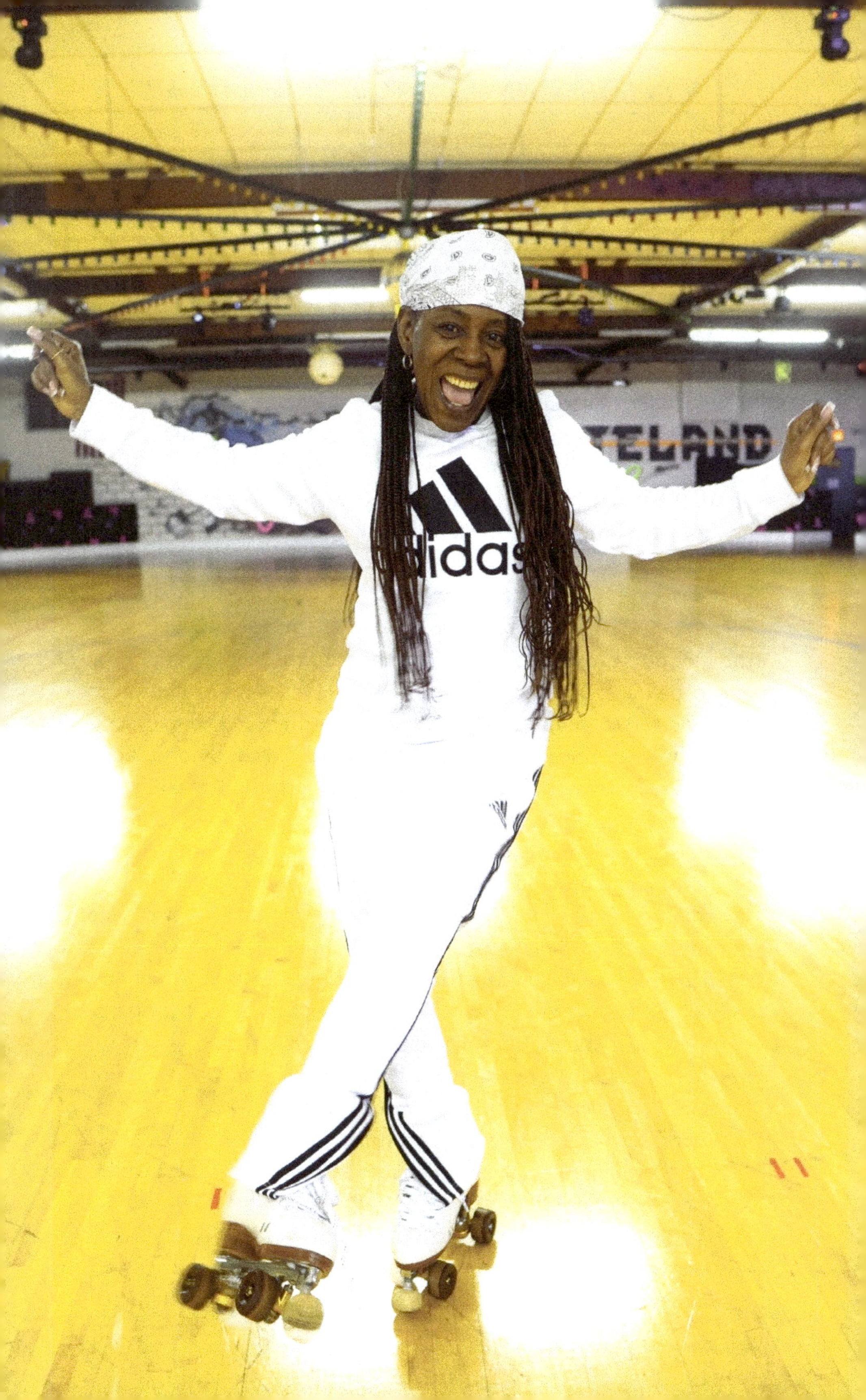

TV in my neighborhood that could receive channel TV 62, and every Saturday we would crowd around this nineteen-inch color TV and take turns holding the antenna to get reception and keep a decent picture. Afterward, we would rush to the school gym and would attempt to mimic all the intricate skating moves we saw.

My overwhelming feeling to "JUST SKATE" took another turn when a roller-skating rink was finally built in the inner city of Flint called Rolletts Skating Arena. This is when I had to learn that one's life continues to evolve and the old are often replaced with the new. I was devastated and, at the same time, ecstatic. My childhood skating crew no longer had an interest in following the art of roller skating and I had to move on without them and find a new crew.

Rolletts had a grand opening and skating was open almost every day of the week. During that first week, skaters from every neighborhood came, and we were introduced to a group of skaters from Detroit called the Detroit Travelin' Rollers. The founder of the club, Regina Ramsey, would invite, sponsor, coach, and train us. We were in Detroit every weekend and sometimes during the week, getting exposed to other great skaters with terrific routines and attitudes to match. Being exposed to the different facets included the history of Detroit roller skating. Even though I'd won my first skating competition in a gym in the third grade, this is where my competitive spirit was truly born. I had to be the best I could be. Competitions where almost every week in Detroit, my athleticism along with the proficiency of my musicality to emerge. My individualism heightened, and I felt empowered to succeed, now realizing that pairs, couples, trios, and skate clubs were all a bonus to individual skating. What I found out was I needed to be proficient in my individual skating and discipline. Now roller skating was saving my life, and I didn't even know it. Things were going on around me in my community and I did not even see it happening or coming. I was sick with it!! Everything I did had to revolve around skating. To this very day, I still apply that same concept to how I live. God, family, and skating, in that order!

At the time, I did not realize that Flint was in its own crisis. My city was embalmed and powered by the epidemic of crack cocaine. This epidemic paralyzed our small city, changing it into a landfill.

Roller skating popularity increased, but our skating rink closed because of unwarranted violence. It was only opened for three years. When I returned home from college for the summer break, I searched for old friends but found new ones and never returned to school. By this time, we had moved back to our original rink in Mt. Morris, Michigan, and I was skating my ass off. So glad to be amongst peers getting it in every Wednesday night. My mom worked relentlessly for GM and my dad considered himself the "entrepreneur" of the family, who ran a small drug operation from Saginaw, Michigan, to Shreveport, Louisiana. Even though Mom had divorced him in 1970, she always allowed us the privilege of knowing our father despite her reservations. That is my dad. I loved him. Whatever I could do for him, I did and before I knew it, not only was I selling drugs, I was using them as well. Now ninety percent of everyone I knew was affiliated some kind of way with the game. Gradually, skate sessions no longer had the numbers they once did. As I mentioned earlier, some rinks closed. We (addicts) were losing interest in skating, skaters were going to school, starting families, and simply relocating to pursue a better life. I intentionally stayed away from the current skaters because of embarrassment from what I allowed the drugs/money to do to me. Now, I am in the full lifestyle of drugs and shenanigans. Shenanigans is the stuff you do to get the drugs when the money runs out.

The population in Flint was over 190,000. At least five hundred to six hundred people at the rink every week and everybody was looking for the same thing, a good time, with or without the skates! Everyone worked for General Motors. We never went without, but if there was any lack, it was definitely temporary. We kept the latest gear, the newest cars. You could not tell us nothing! Years passed quickly as the drugs gradually took over and plagued families and communities from every walk of life. I gave up my quest for skating because crack cocaine and skating just do not match. Crack was winning. It is like trying to fit a square peg in a round hole. It doesn't work. Now it is a huge problem and at this point, I am desperately trying to find myself...by any means necessary! We watched the dope dealers get richer as everyone else suffered from addiction. It was like a movie! In order to get a grip, I moved to the city of Milwaukee, where my dad had found success in recovery and legal business ventures as well. The same route I took to get involved in this was the same to get out. *My dad!* That is where my recovery process began. I entered a rehabilitation center that specialized in the recovery process for Black women in the summer of 1999. The program was simple, but the process was real! My parents never left my side. Everybody giving up on me and counting me out was the incentive that fueled me. With hard work and pure determination, I let the miracle happen. Once I understood what role I played in my demise, things made a lot more sense.

I was working on myself now! Grasping that I was in full-blown recovery and ready to roll again, but I was not in Michigan, and that was a problem, so I thought. I did not know anyone who skated or if they even had a rink, but I found one! When I got there, there were only about twenty-five people which made me think that there was not any skating history in this town and no one had any interest in it, but I was wrong. This city had suffered the same crisis as any other city and their skating scene was on the comeback as well. So, this is the part of the story where skating saves my life again. I no longer even owned a pair of skates. I had to rock the rentals. After two weeks of that, I was calling home to buy Fomac wheels, placing orders for boots and plates. This particular rink wasn't familiar with the social media skating sites, so as I met people, I shared about that, and they listened. Skate crews/groups formed, they traveled to other cities and states. Of course, I went and had a good time. Traveling south was always my favorite. I would spend the most time with Charles Haywood, being as studious as possible. He was truly the best and his passing angered me to no end. When I participated in the WSA competitions while in Georgia, he would come and support me and was also pleased to see me judging this genre of skating (jam skating). Let it be known. I never aborted the Michigan style of skating. Wherever I competed, I did me! Even skating world class. What a blessing!

A small group of skaters from Milwaukee accompanied me to New York for the movie premier of *Roll Bounce*. How cool was that! 'Cause when Tyrone Dixon called me for the movie, I called my hitters from Detroit. It was an awesome learning experience... memorable! At this time, I was fortunate enough to have a lunch meeting at a small restaurant on the Northside of Chicago with Mr. Bill Butler. After lunch, when we went to his sister's home, I watched hours of video of him explaining his skating technique. He described it as Syncopated Rhythmic Movement. Well years later, the skate style heavily resembles Snappin' (in my opinion) and we all know that's Poppin'! He was also ecstatic about his skaters having the leading roles in the movie. And so was I.

Now that I was a responsible adult with a vision and plan, I desperately wanted to go home. The year 2009 and the population of one hundred forty thousand, the rink has approximately two hundred skaters per week. People were migrating quickly from the city again because of the downsizing of General Motors. At this time, Flint was known for the highest crime rate and repeatedly ranked number for one of the most dangerous cities in the United States of America. Knowing the economics in Michigan was not best and that I would go from better to worst, I left anyway. Leaving the family business and the security of knowing how all my financial needs were going to be met was the new challenge. The evolution continues!

The vibe in the rink was cool in Flint, but different. I did not see it coming. Another generation of skaters had entered the scene. The music was changing also. It almost felt like seasons changing with no protection from the weather. I was not prepared for the change. After years of injuries, my knees just were not ready for what I wanted to do. My body was physically tired. Our style of skating can be very demanding on your entire body and after years of competing, not allowing the injuries to heal before I was in the next competition was catching up to me. You must control your weight and muscle tone to keep that low game popping! We do drops, half drops, side splits, shoot the ducks on a regular. That is when you know you are getting older when those moves become more challenging. This shit had caught up with me where it hurt the most and the real pain began. My thoughts were telling me, *This is it, my competing days are over.* Now I was just existing at the rink. The pain became excruciating. I could no longer take it...I quit! Diagnosis: rheumatoid arthritis. I still was not realizing that all the physical therapy in the world could not prepare me for what was next.

My head was telling me one thing, but my body said something is else. Picking up weight that I could not even explain because I had never been a huge eater. I tried working out regularly with absolutely no results. Every task became prolonged. I would dress for skating but not go. I did not have the interest or energy after preparation. Smells were coming from the kitchen and bathroom, but from where? Hair was thinning, nails were brittle and my skin felt like sandpaper. Smells we could not identify soon turned to cloudy water, water even coming out of our faucets like bubbles. April 2014…we had feces in our water and large amounts of lead. They were trying to kill us! The entire city of Flint was now in a water crisis and we had no clean water anywhere. You could not cook with it, drink or bathe. Where they do that at? Flint! Look, to make a long story short, people left the city; celebrities, companies, communities, water came from everywhere. Filters, filtration systems, and lead tests were offered as well. Street by street, new pipes leading to our homes were replaced. But the damage had already been done. We do not knowingly drink water from anyone's faucet, period. To get through the process of being poisoned by water, I had to become an alkaline plant-based eater. And before I knew it, I was skating World Class events coached by Carlesa Williams. My confidence was back; even those were the worst performances of my career.

Population now less than ninety thousand. Ghost. 2015, our rink was feeling the financial burden of the water crisis. Our morale was low, thirty to forty skaters every Wednesday night, faithfully for the next four years! I could not stop skating. I needed to skate. Skating never gave up on me. I was determined to stay as long as they kept the doors open. On September 4, 2019, a young entrepreneur name Terrance Carter gave a skating party and invited three hundred of his closest friends, and guess what? They never left. We rolling y'all! Flint's resilience is totally awesome and we are never to be counted out. We represent and share a long roller-skating heritage with Detroit, Michigan.

Eight months later, the entire world was on lockdown and I was totally devastated that we couldn't skate, not knowing how severe this pandemic actually was. I woke up one day, and I heard something in my spirit saying, *Shoot a video.* I didn't ponder with the idea I just did it. Well, in order to do that you need a song. Met with some people and we recorded a song titled "Just Skate." The concept of the video was to include as many skaters as I could despite location. Through Quad Lovers Sk8 Entertainment, Cynthia and I got skaters from Africa, Italy, France, Barcelona, California, Texas, Tennessee, Detroit, Flint, Portugal, and Chicago. I simply wanted all genres of roller skating to participate in this project. First to give skaters a platform to shine, secondly to show solidarity and love to the rest of the world because we rolling through this pandemic with both barrels smokin'. I had to get creative. We took advantage of every opportunity, location, and sunny day we could to make this happen. I am grateful!!

The art of starting over is a continual process in my neck of the woods. Surviving a cocaine epidemic, water crisis, a pandemic, and everything else that life throws at us, we continue to "Just Skate." I refer to the term "we" meaning all those who encourage me. I could not have done it by myself…

All those who respect the process of maintaining and preserving our roller-skating culture, blessing one another on and off the skating floor, make us unbreakable. Support and respect all genres of skating. It is enough to go around! Have fun, may God bless your soul with the opportunity to "JUST SKATE."

## Do You Know...

### Longest Travel on Roller Skates

The Guinness World Record for the longest distance traveled on roller skates in 24 hours epitomizes the endurance and determination of roller skaters. Participants undertake a grueling challenge, skating continuously for an entire day to cover as much ground as possible within the allotted time frame. Preparation is key, with skaters meticulously planning their route, pacing, and rest breaks to optimize performance.

Skaters must adhere to strict guidelines and documentation requirements set by Guinness World Records officials. This includes using certified equipment to accurately measure the distance skated and having witnesses and timekeepers present to verify progress. The record attempt is not only a physical feat but also a mental test, with skaters pushing through fatigue and monotony to achieve their goal.

Throughout the 24-hour period, skaters face physical and mental challenges, including fatigue and muscle soreness. However, fueled by their passion for roller skating and the desire to make history, they persevere. With each completed lap, they edge closer to surpassing the existing record, driven by the pursuit of excellence and the thrill of breaking new ground.

Upon completion of the 24-hour challenge, the skater's total distance skated is meticulously measured and documented. If successful, the skater earns the prestigious title of Guinness World Record holder, solidifying their place in roller skating history and inspiring others to push their limits.

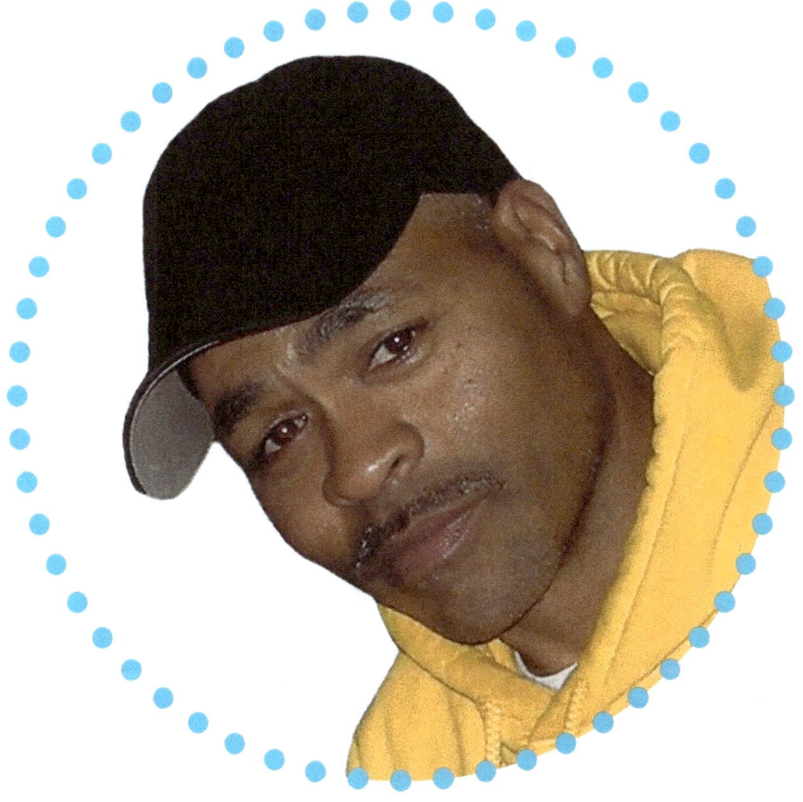

Ron Butts

aka G Wiz

Facebook: @Gee Wiz | Instagram: @theoriginalgwiz

## "My Fascination with Music"

I began my career in the music industry. A lover of R&B, soul, and hip-hop music, I was tuned into them as a youngster, so I started a neighborhood street band. I recall our instruments were basically household items or any object that made noise. Still, it was entertainment for those who could stand to listen. My fascination with music composition, beats, and lyrics inspired me to write a five-volume collection of my favorite songs in notebooks. I figured if I couldn't sing, I would at least know the words to the songs, taking notice of those who incorrectly sang the wrong lines during a performance. By high school graduation, I was interested in spinning records to entertain those who like to party.

Grand Wizard is the original name I selected as my DJ handle, which I shortened to G Wiz. Heavily influenced by Grand Master Flash, Grand Wizard Theodore a New York DJ who created the "needle dropping" technique, Philadelphia D.J. Jazzy Jeff's cutting and scratching, and New York DJ/producer Marley Marl's mixing, I created a signature style that entertains wherever I am laying down the sounds. I keep the music hyped at parties, during broadcasting, and the roller rink, where I continue to spin on occasion. I successfully produced music video shows and dance party mixes that received local and national recognition. As the former owner and producer of Wiz-A-Tron Records and CEO of Street Vibes Videos, I established affiliations with Atlantic, Interscope, and Def Jam Record Companies, marketing my creation of the Video Mix. I started the concept of laying video footage on top of audio recordings of my radio broadcast while critiquing the show. Soon it became a big demand to match random video scenes to the words of songs.

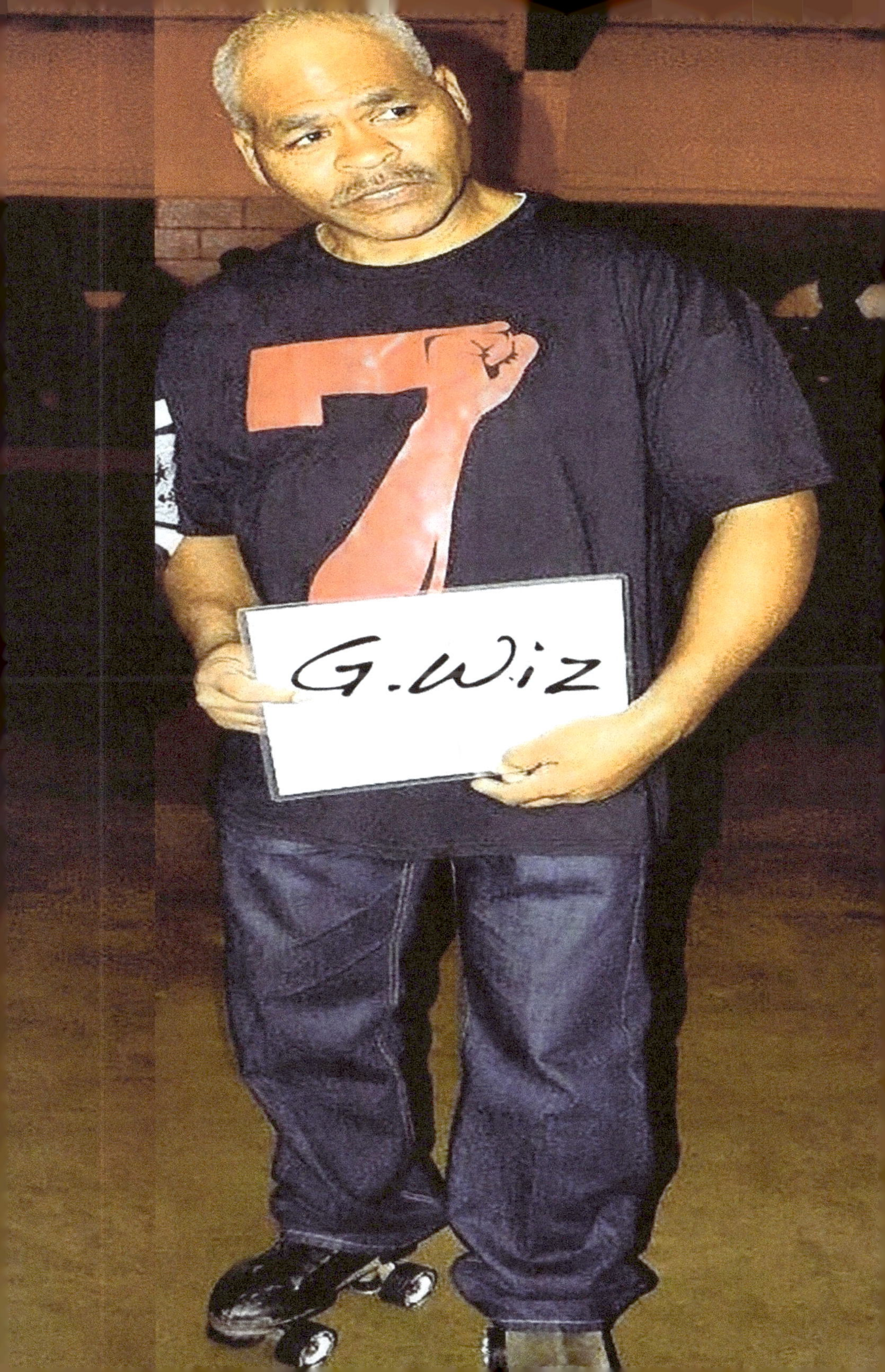
G.Wiz

My first video editing was utilizing the standard A/B roll off line editing. Then I advanced to non-linear computer editing with Adobe Premier, Avid Express, and on to Final Cut Pro. I admit that I am a novice documentary filmmaker with so much more to learn. Still, I am determined to take my love for entertainment and the art of film to another level. The first documentary I co-produced titled, *Ruff Cutts,* is about the evolution of hip-hop and rap music. *The Rink*, my second documentary, pays respect to legendary roller skaters in St. Louis, Mo, and East St. Louis, IL. My latest is a three-part documentary series, *Background Check*, based on the early days of St. Louis, Mo, and East St. Louis, IL hip-hop. This documentary is another link in the chain of projects yet to come. My aspiration is to be an Urban Documentary Filmmaker, specializing in the positive aspects of the Black Experience.

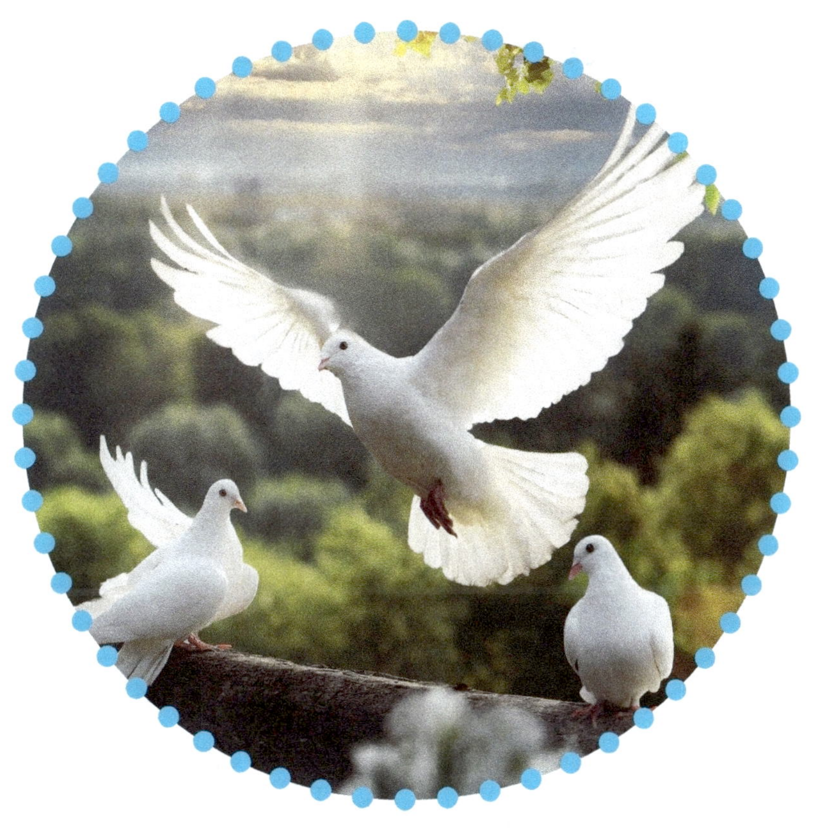

# In Memoriam

# *"Gone But Not Forgotten"*

*"We all die.*
*The goal isn't to live forever,*
*the goal is to create something that will.*
~Chuck Palaniuk

## *A Tribute to Scott T. Randolph, aka Slo Motion*

Excerpted from his unpublished work
*Head Over Wheels*
*(Authorized by Corinne Dayon)*

## How I Fell in Love with Roller Skating...

We were four teenage boys that could barely keep our balance on a pair of roller skates. We held on to the guardrail or each other for dear life, playing a game of tag, speeding around the floor with our arms flailing about and falling, often in laughter. We skated faster than any beginner skaters should. We were fearless. We did not care what anyone thought or how anyone looked at us. We were out to have fun and 'fun' is exactly what it was. This was my introduction to Empire Roller Disco during the summer of 1977.

Back then, we rented our skates, and a decent pair of rentals became vital. To do that, we had to slip a few bucks to the guy behind the rental

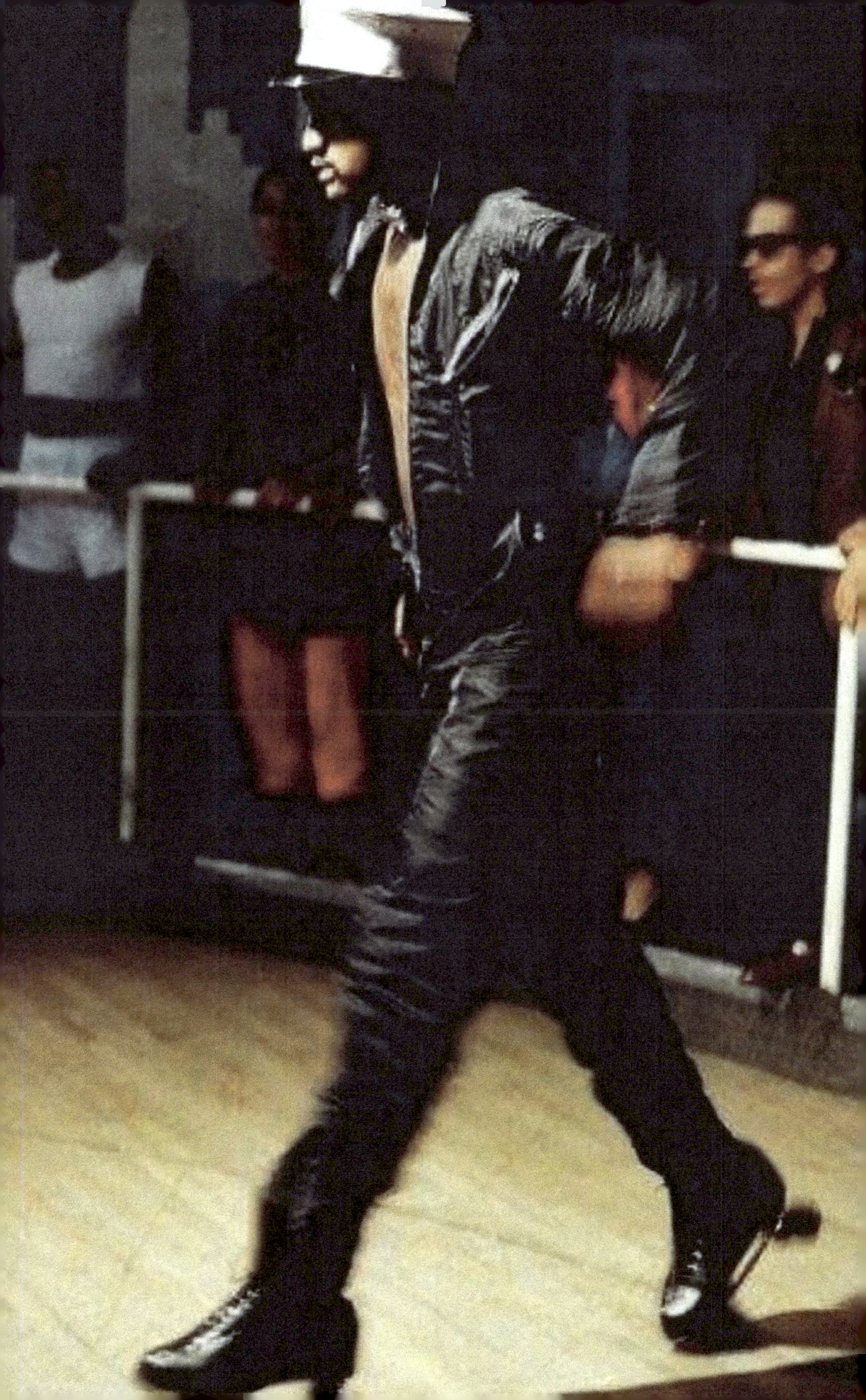

counter. No matter how new those rentals were, we always got blisters the next day. I would go as often as I could with my cousins to watch the girls and listen to the clear, bass-bouncing music. At some point, they lost interest and stopped going as often. But for me, the experience was so amazing that I knew I found my passion. Falling in love with roller skating was instantaneous. It was love at first flight. There was nothing better on Earth. Floating on the wood to the music.

One day, I woke up with my muscles aching and my legs throbbing, my blistered feet and my back hurting, and I loved it. I didn't mind any of the pain. Because for the first time, I felt free. Only a true skater or someone who has found their passion being on eight wheels will understand that statement. Even after hours and hours of intense, relentless practicing spins kicks, jumps, turns and every possible trick you can think of, I wanted more. No matter how tired you are, no matter how much pain your body is in, no matter how much sweat you have produced, you still want more. Even when your body can't go any further and the music stops and they are turning the lights off in the rink, you still want more. Even when you are tired and know you need to go to sleep, you still want more. I could not wait until the sun came up. I craved more time to skate. That's when I knew I had fallen head over wheels in love with roller skating.

In 2020, we lost Scott 'Slo Mo' during the COVID lockdown. Scott and I share a daughter and three granddaughters. Scott and I have always cherished the memories we shared of the many days and nights we spent together skating the streets of NYC. The Skate Circle will always be our "home," which is why our family will bury his ashes this fall at the original Skate Circle.

Today, Wayne Bradley has a designated space of his own located away from today's circle. He spends time repairing cracks and keeping what he so passionately created alive.

As for the original founders of the Central Park Skate Circle, this is our legacy. RIP Scott Randolph

—Corrine Dayon

## CENTRAL PARK SKATE CIRCLE—OUR LEGACY

It was the summer of 1980 on a hot, muggy summer night in New York City. As we did every night, it was after another night of skating at Roxy, a group of us roller skaters would make our way to the flat marble floor of the Time and Life Building on Avenue of the Americas, across from Radio City Music Hall. With several Boom Boxes playing the same radio station, we would roll until the sun came up, and either made our way home to sleep or go to work without sleep. Some of us would separate and skate into Central Park to the Goodskates pavilion. On this one early morning skate was when we spotted city workers paving the 'flats,' which originally was dirt, to make way for volleyball courts. As all skaters know, finding a smooth pavement is a skater's dream. Now I can't remember everyone present because it was forty years ago, but Scott "Slo Motion" Randolph and Wayne Bradley came up with the idea to buy spray paint and paint a circle. Placing a few Boom Boxes in the center, the Skate Circle was born.

It's been four decades and there have been changes. The Skate Circle today has none of the original founders. It isn't even in the original spot. It is regulated by the CPDSA and Bob Nichols. From what I understand, former Mayor Rudy Giuliani had tried to get rid of the skate circle in the nineties, and for roller skaters to continue to skate, the CPDSA was created.

## Do You Know...

### The Most Spins While on Roller Skates

The Guinness World Record for the most spins while roller skating in one minute is a remarkable demonstration of balance, agility, and precision. Skaters attempting this record aim to execute as many rotations as possible within a 60-second timeframe, showcasing their mastery of spinning techniques on roller skates. Achieving this record requires not only exceptional skating skills but also intense focus and control to maintain momentum and stability throughout the rapid spins.

Preparation is crucial for skaters gearing up to attempt this record. They must train rigorously to perfect their spinning technique, honing their balance and timing to execute fast and controlled rotations. Practicing spins on a regular basis helps skaters develop the muscle memory and coordination needed to perform at their best during the record attempt. Additionally, skaters may experiment with different types of spins, such as one-foot spins or multiple rotations in succession, to maximize their spin count.

During the record attempt, skaters must maintain a steady rhythm and tempo to maximize their spin count while ensuring each rotation is completed cleanly and without loss of balance. The skater's ability to generate and sustain rotational momentum is critical, as any hesitation or wobbling could disrupt the flow of spins and hinder their chances of breaking the record. Mental focus is paramount, with skaters channeling their concentration and determination into each spin to achieve their maximum potential.

As the clock ticks down, the pressure mounts for the skater to maintain their pace and rhythm until the final second. With each rotation completed, they edge closer to surpassing the existing record, propelled by the adrenaline of the moment and the desire to leave their mark in roller skating history. Upon completion of the one-minute timeframe, the skater's total spin count is meticulously tallied and verified by Guinness World Records officials. If successful, the skater earns the prestigious title of Guinness World Record holder, showcasing their exceptional skill and talent in the realm of roller skating spins.

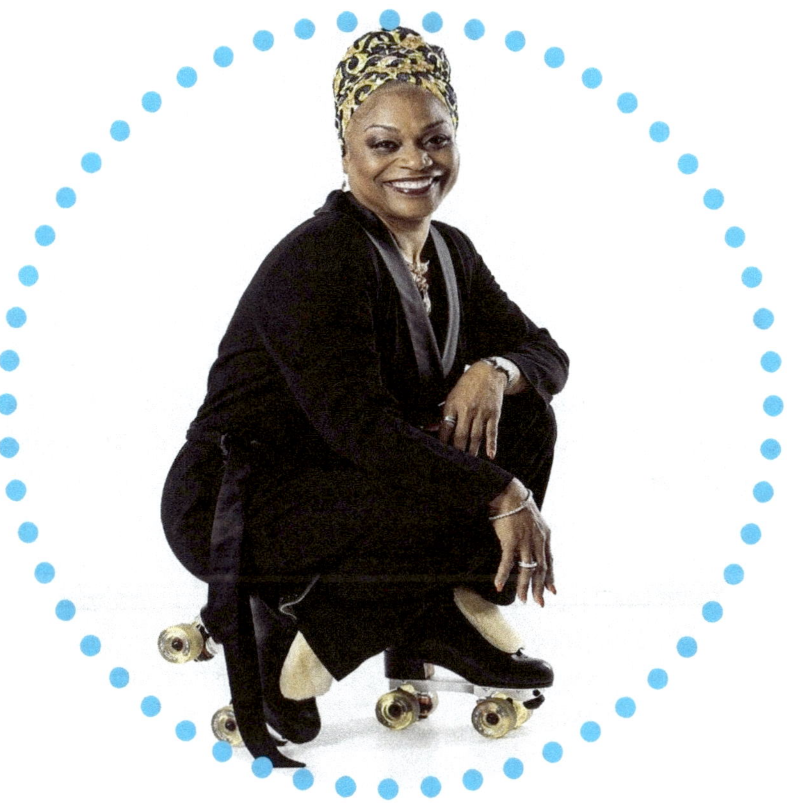

# Amirah Palmer

Facebook: @Amirah Palmer | Instagram: @itsamirahpalmer

# "About the Lead Author"

Amirah Palmer is not just a skater; she is a visionary, serial entrepreneur, and the founder and CEO of Sk8rz Konnect. Her platform, Sk8rz Konnect, serves as a showcase for the diverse skills and artistry found in various forms of skating, including roller, ice, and skateboarding. Amirah is a decorated U.S. Army Veteran, an International Best Selling Author, and a graduate of the University of Maryland. Her passion extends to volunteering and community service.

Through The Evolution of Skating series, Amirah Palmer aims to create a unified platform that brings together every genre of the skating arts. Her goal is to connect, showcase, and inspire skaters in their respective fields, fostering a sense of community and encouragement within the skating world.

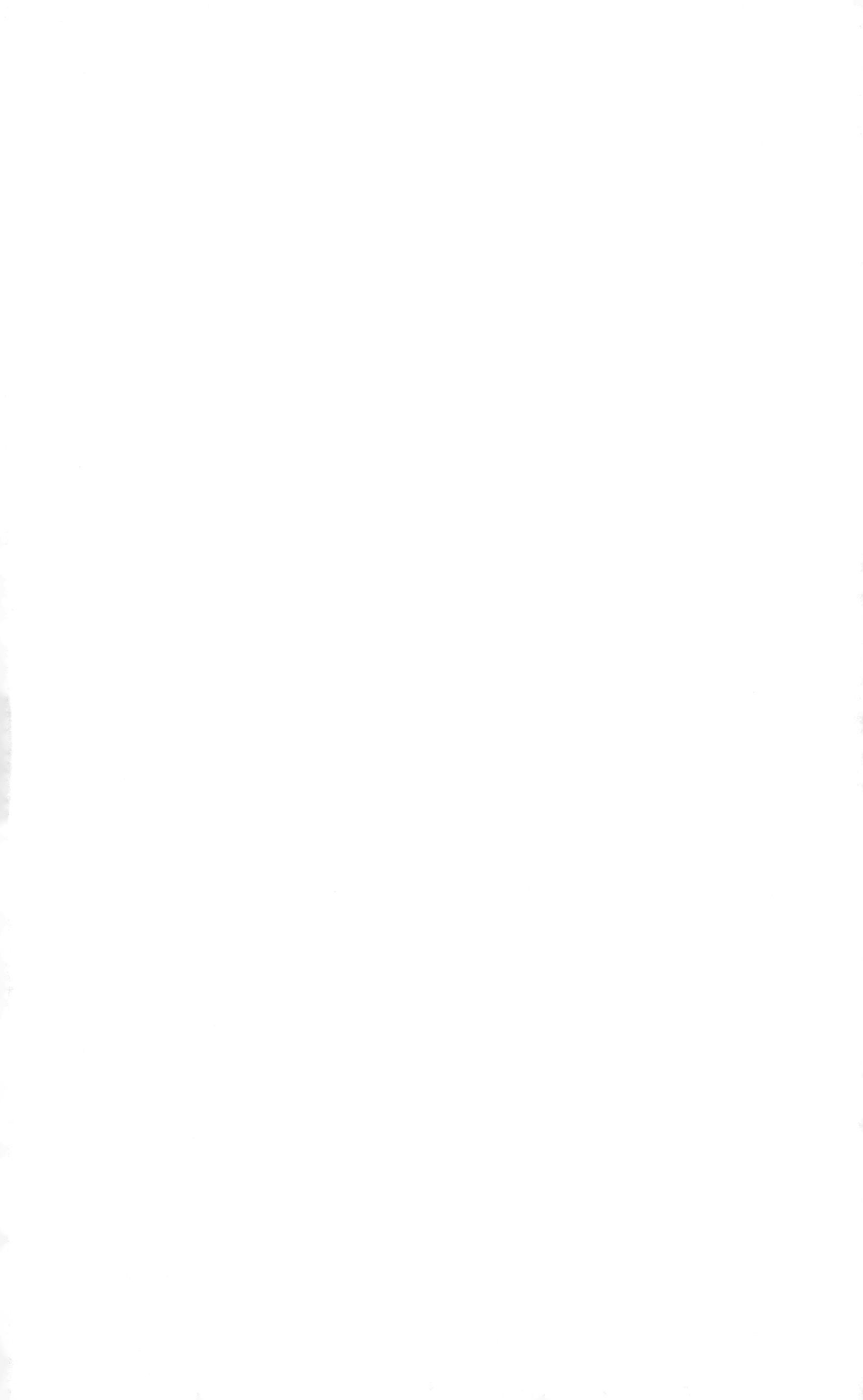

www.ingramcontent.com/pod-product-compliance
Lightning Source LLC
LaVergne TN
LVHW010608110826
845149LV00003B/826

* 9 7 9 8 9 9 0 4 9 7 5 3 5 *